JELLY ROLL MORTON'S LAST NIGHT AT THE JUNGLE INN

JELLY ROLL MORTON'S LAST NIGHT AT THE JUNGLE INN

An Imaginary Memoir by
SAMUEL CHARTERS

Marion Boyars
New York London

Published in the United States and Great Britain in 1984 by
MARION BOYARS INC.
457 Broome Street, New York 10013
Distributed in the United States by
The Scribner Book Companies Inc.
and
MARION BOYARS LTD
18 Brewer Street, London W1R 4AS

Distributed in Canada by
John Wiley and Sons Canada Ltd

Distributed in Australia and New Zealand by
Thomas C. Lothian Pty Ltd

Library of Congress Cataloging in Publication Data
Charters, Samuel Barclay.
  Jelly Roll Morton's last night at the Jungle Inn.
  1. Morton, Jelly Roll, d. 1941—Fiction.
  I. Title.
PS3553.H327J4 1984 813'.54 83-11777

British Library Cataloguing in Publication Data
Charters, Samuel
  Jelly Roll Morton's last night at the Jungle Inn.
  I. Title.
  813'.54[F] PS3553.H/

ISBN 0-7145-2805-6 cloth

Manufactured in the USA

Set in 12 on 14 Goudy Old Style
By Top Type

For Frederic Ramsey Jr.
and for Amelia

*Like so many others, I couldn't have begun myself
without the books you created, your photographs, and all
that you shared with me when – with Amelia and Annie
– we talked those nights through so many years ago.*

A NOTE

Jelly Roll Morton was born in 1885 and died in 1941, so I never had a chance to hear him play or listen to him talk, but I grew up with his recordings and the autobiographical monologs he put on disc for the Library of Congress. I used to dream about what it might have been like to sit at a table with him and listen to him talk when he finished playing for the night. For a long time I thought of writing a book about Jelly Roll's life and career, and I interviewed a number of people and began to gather material. In the end, however, I finally realized that what I wanted to know about him were the personal things — the stories, reminiscences, and anecdotes; as well as the exaggerations, justifications, and lies. This book is the story I thought Jelly Roll might have told me if I had ever been able to meet him at the Jungle Inn.

The outline of his life, as he relates it here, follows what is known about him very closely. He was an adolescent in New Orleans during the Robert Charles riots in 1900, and he traveled to Pensacola, New York, Los Angeles, and Chicago during the periods described in the book. There was no honky tonk called Boodie's in Pensacola, as far as I know, but Wilkin's cabaret in New York was an actual place. Jelly Roll's description of his performance there, however, is fictitious. The names of the piano players he describes in Pensacola are also fictitious, however the other musicians mentioned in the book, and the roles they played in Jelly Roll's story, are real. During the Depression, when the royalties from his recordings dried up, he managed a night club in Washington, D. C. It had several names, the last of which was The Jungle Inn.

Two of the women in the book, Anita Gonzales and Mabel Bertrand, were real persons, and the descriptions of his life with them are factual. The other two women and their stories are fictitious. Jelly Roll once mentioned a waitress in Mexico who inspired the title of his piece "The Pearls," and in the late 1920s he recorded a piece named after a woman whom he called "Mississippi Mildred." Perhaps it was they who were "Mildred" and "Rose."

S.C.

JELLY ROLL MORTON'S
LAST NIGHT AT
THE JUNGLE INN

I certainly want to thank you for coming around to the club here to listen to my music. An artist always appreciates it when folks come around and it's very, very nice when they want to sit down like this and talk and have a little drink. This is very lovely whiskey and I certainly appreciate you leaving the bottle on the table here. Of course there have been a lot of parties, people coming to hear me play and bringing their friends and booking agents and managers and so forth and so on. It always is that way when you have something to offer the people and I always have had something to offer which they couldn't get from nobody else. If it's jazz music you're thinking about, when you come to see Jelly Roll Morton you don't need to go no further because I'm the one that invented it. I am the one that started it all. Of course you know that. When you come here the first time and we sat talking I told you all about that and I know you were listening because you got a pair of ears and you don't use them just to keep your hat off the end of your nose.

This being the last night and all, I want you to know I really do appreciate it that you're down here to listen. Oftentimes an artist can be up there in front of the public and he can be doing everything in the line of entertaining for that public and it goes right past

9

them. They don't see what he's bringing to them. They don't catch it. Well, I've had some nights playing piano here where I thought that was going to happen to me. Of course, I always did have the crowd that come to hear what I had to offer, big spenders and people like that. All kinds of people. But you can't expect to have that every night. I don't think any artist every had that. I know there was some nights when Enrico Caruso said to himself I never should have come out on this stage. The public isn't getting what I'm doing. Here I am giving them all my talent and it's not going over. I know there was nights when the great Louis Armstrong, when Bing Crosby didn't have nobody to listen to them. I know for a fact there's some nights when everybody in the country's too tired to turn on the radio. That's when all them boys, I don't care who they are, they might as well never open their mouths because there's nobody that's going to listen. I've had those nights myself right here in this club. Of course I don't say it's the greatest club you'd ever want to set foot in. The fact of the matter is, it's a dump. So I understand that it has to be something else that brings you down here. I appreciate you coming around to listen to what it is I have to present. Of course I also appreciate you staying around to talk a little before you go. It gets hot up at the piano there, what with the lights and so many people crowding around and I have to take a little time to get back to my own self.

People say to me sometimes, Jelly, you talk too much. They say if you could just attach up your mouth to a machine you would be a millionaire because your mouth never stops moving, but I say to them you see an animal in the zoo and you don't hear it talking. You see the little bitty monkeys running around in their cages and they don't have a thing to say. You see a mule hitched up to a wagon and you can stand there looking at that mule until the sun goes down and you won't hear a word. If a man can't talk he's no better than an animal. Now you take a man like me who is out on the road and spends so many days and nights in hotels and rooming houses and boarding houses and sitting down to eat breakfast in a restaurant somewhere with a newspaper to read and waiting for the club to open where you supposed to play piano. No matter who you are you look around you sometime and you see it's very quiet. And when it gets quiet like that it helps you to hear somebody talking. It helps you even if you're the one that's doing it. I have been so many places and done so many things pertaining to show business and gambling and so forth and so on. I could stay up all night and I never would have to tell the same story twice. You have heard me when I was describing all the different things which have happened to me and you know what I'm telling you is the truth.

So many people come up to me and want to know my story. Every kind of people you can name and they want to know about me. Sometimes they try to get a little tough with me and they say, what you doing in a two-bit place like this if you're such a big shot, and I come back at them by asking, boy, where you been since your mother wiped you dry? Don't you know this is 1940 and times is hard, and as far as this being such a run-down place this is not New York or Hollywood, this is Washington, D.C. and you have to expect that things will be a little different here. What we have endeavored to do in the Jungle

11

Inn is to entertain the people and I believe we have succeeded in that line.

Of course there is no man living who doesn't have a story to his life and I suppose you might say one part of my story is the inside of all these clubs and cabarets and honky tonks where I have played piano. Now I say that's my story because I commenced when I was just a little boy. It wasn't my intention that I would grow up like this, but I don't think there's a man living who knew when he started just where he would end up. I can see you're still very young and you no doubt haven't begun to think about what you will do with yourself, but the truth is, whatever you think you going to do, you damn sure going to wind up doing something else. I started off in the honky tonks when I was so young because I was not given a choice in the matter. I come from a Creole family which goes far back in history in New Orleans and they didn't approve of my being a piano player. If I made it my choice to go on playing piano in those low kind of places, I couldn't remain at home. So you are sitting with a man who has been on the move all his life. The fact is, you could say another part of the story of my life is being on the move. I suppose I'm just like a lot of other people. Once you start traveling it gets to be kind of a habit and you don't want to stop. That's still the truth about my life today. I can tell you how to start traveling on the road, but I can't tell you how to stop, and the reason for that is I don't know myself.

The truth is, I have played in much worse places than this. After I had to leave home I stayed over with my godmother in Biloxi, Mississippi, which is over on the Gulf Coast, and it was from there that I commenced my traveling. And that has taken me into places so bad that I don't think if you went there even today that the police themselves would dare to set foot in the door for fear someone would take their heads off. It didn't make no difference who they were, if they didn't look right they didn't get in or out that door. I got in, of course, because of my ability to play piano, but if the place was too rough I wouldn't say anything about that right at first. Most any place I could get in the door because, like I said, I've always been known to be a fair talker and when I'd get in the door I'd kind of hang around until I could hear the fellow that was in the place play a little. Then I would know what I was up against. I wanted to let the other fellow play first to kind of feel him out, what kind of tunes the fellow would go for and so forth and so on.

I remember one night in a little bit of a honky tonk kind of place outside of Pensacola, Florida. That was about 1904, in the early part of the year. I was nineteen years old and still wasn't nothing but a boy though of course I thought I was a man, and I had all those kind of simple girls after me because I had already began to be a fancy dresser. Anyway, my clothes didn't look like much that night because I had taken a lift with a fellow from Mobile, Alabama, who had a job delivering oysters to a big restaurant in Pensacola. So I asked him if it was alright if I took a lift from him because I wanted to get to Pensacola. I'd heard about all the piano players they had there and I knew that if they had a lot of piano players they must have a lot of jobs and everything was kind of tight just then in Mobile, so I got this fellow to take me with him when he delivered those oysters.

Now this fellow had a big dog that he had with him all the time, because there was all kind of men down there on the waterfront that would take your money before you could count to one if you didn't have some kind of protection. So he had this big dog with him and I took one look at that dog and that dog took one look at me and we didn't see eye to eye. I tell you if that dog could have gotten to me through the door of the fellow's truck he'd have shooken me up until my arms and legs come off. He'd have bitten me up and down until I had more holes in me than some kind of a sieve that they use in the kitchen. So the fellow says to me, if you want to come along to Pensacola you going to have to ride back there with the oysters because you sure as hell ain't going to ride up here with the dog. I didn't have nothing to say to that and I didn't have enough money to get on the train, so I got up on the back of the truck there and I hunkered down on the sacks with all them oysters. Now oysters, of course, is kind of damp, and they have a smell to them, and after I'd bounced around a little on the back of that fellow's truck you couldn't tell which one of us was smelling worser, the oysters or me, and of course this didn't do my fancy clothes any good. Fact of the matter was that after I got down off that truck people kept looking around when I come past wondering where the fish wagon was at. Only it wasn't any wagon, it was just me.

Anyway, I got off that man's truck in Pensacola and I come to this honky tonk called "Boodie's Place". Now it probably had some other name but I don't remember just what it could be. Boodie was the name of the fellow that was behind the bar so that was what give the name to it. I went there because I had heard that Boodie's was where you went to find the big spenders. I knew if I could get inside the joint I could get myself a pool game or if I couldn't do anything in the pool line I could hustle the piano player. I still had to get the smell of those oyster sacks off me, so I walked around town until I found a fountain and I took my hands and dipped water out of the fountain and wiped off the sleeves of my coat and the backs of my trousers to get some of the oyster smell off me — then I took off for Boodie's.

Of course in those days you had to be careful of where you walked, because the police, well if they saw a colored person being somewhere they didn't think he ought to be they'd have him down in the jail quicker than a cat can jump up a tree. And it was just as hard for him to get out of there. But I stayed where I could see I wouldn't get in no trouble and all I had to do was say the word "Boodie's" and the colored people in that town would just point. Everybody knew where Boodie's was. So I came to Boodie's and they had a fellow on the door named Skinny Walter. Now the reason they gave him the name Skinny was because that man had muscles on him like some kind of picture in a magazine. That man had shoulders on him stronger than Joe Louis, and once you got inside if you got yourself into any kind of trouble you would just look around and Skinny Walter would be coming up, and then you know you really would be in some kind of jam.

Of course, Skinny Walter let me get in the door at the honky tonk there because I gave him a story of some kind. I told him I had a pawn ticket to deliver to one of the gentlemen at the bar or something in that line and Skinny Walter just stood away from the door and let me come in 'cause he figured if I did get in any kind of trouble I was such a skinny little fellow that I wouldn't do nobody no harm. Now they had everything in the line of drinks there, but what kept the place going was the games. I don't know what kind of games were allowed in Pensacola at that time, but police was never known to get closer than two corners away from Boodie's and when they even started coming in that direction they sent a little boy running ahead to tell everybody they were coming so the fellows would have time to clear out and there wouldn't be no kind of trouble. So they didn't give the police any kind of thought inside of the place. Of all the games in history there wasn't a one of them you couldn't find there in one of the back rooms. They had craps and they had skin and they had blackjack and they had so many poker games going on you couldn't count all the guys that lost their money there every night. Of course I was just there for the piano player seeing as how I didn't have any money and my clothes was still all wet where I'd wiped myself to get the smell of the oysters off.

Now there had been many famous piano players from Pensacola. Everybody has heard of the world famous Pensacola Kid and they had many others there who could give the piano a run for its money. There was players like Louis Amory who knew all the Scott Joplin numbers and One-Eye Carl who had lost his right eye in a shooting accident when somebody had accidentally caught him holding onto a card when the deal was going on. One-Eye Carl played all those songs people liked to hear at the time. He wasn't in a class with Tony Jackson or Louis Chauvin, but there wasn't a piano player in the world who was in a class

16

with those two gentlemen except for myself and I was still just a kid and people didn't want to give me credit for what I could do. For blues they had Arthur Seminole who looked like an Indian and Molasses Johnny and Harry Teacher. Harry could play you any kind of song you wanted to hear, but all he wanted to play was them blues. They all played a simpler kind of blues than you hear nowadays. Just one chord with a lot of notes in the right hand to make you think they really could play. Of course it was the singing that was the most important to them. What they couldn't play they could sing. Now you take Molasses Johnny. They gave him that name because his skin was just about the color of molasses, but I thought they could just as well call him that for the sweet singing voice he had. I tell you he sang those blues so sweet sometimes you'd feel like wiping yourself off when he got finished. I didn't put myself in a class with them when it came to singing a blues tune, but I could sing any other kind of number and when it came down to the piano playing I could do anything they could do and a lot more.

Now when I got inside Boodie's I could hear the piano player in the back room and he didn't have anything. I mean to tell you, I could take you up to that piano there and give you one lesson and you could play more piano than that fellow could. His name was Bill. I never learned his second name but I'm sure he had one. I only knew him as Bill though I was there hanging around for two or three months and he stayed on in the place trying to learn some of my tricks. Now when I got back to the piano I could see that Bill had something going for him because he had all these simple girls doing all kinds of kicks and

shakes while he played. Boodie's was such a wide-open kind of joint that they didn't care what they were showing and they'd throw their legs up in the air and let you get a good look, then they'd jump around a little more so they could wiggle their asses, then they'd hold their legs up in the air again.

All of this made Bill kind of chesty so he was wearing a suit and he had a nice clean shirt and a necktie with a stick pin. Of course with some of those illiterate women it was important to look like you didn't care about nothing, so this Bill had his shirt collar busted open and his tie pulled down so you could discern the top of his red underwear. That was the big thing in New Orleans. All the real fancy dressers there busted open their collars and undid the top buttons of their shirts so you could see their red flannel underwear and somehow Bill had gotten wind of that so he had unbuttoned his shirt a little bit and let the simpler women see what he had on underneath it.

Anyway, I let Bill play. I was enjoying myself looking at all those girls with their legs up in the air and after he played one note I knew I could beat his ass on the piano, so I wasn't worried. After a time he noticed me hanging around and he asked me what I wanted and I asked him could I sing a number along with him. Now I could see that he was kind of proud and if you got a proud fellow that is a fellow you can make a fool out of. Anyway, one or two of the girls had noticed me when I went up to him and they was smiling a little bit because I was so young and even with the damp places from the water I had on nice clothes, and when he saw that they was interested he said, what song do you want to sing? Now I knew all I

19

had to do was to get him to try some song so I looked as innocent as I knew how and I gave him the name of one of the numbers that was in style at that time. "All That I Need Is Love," or some such. And when the girls heard that they said they wanted to hear that number; so I sang one or two lines so they could hear that I had some kind of a voice and that I knew the words. So Bill had to try to play it. I let him go ahead and then I said I'm sorry but that's not the right way to play that number. You don't have the right chords.

So Bill stood up very slowly and said, alright, if you know so much about how this number should go why don't you sit down and play it for us. When Bill said that all the girls started laughing because there wasn't nobody in the place knew I could play. Of course all I wanted to do was get him up off that piano stool so I could sit down.

I let him walk away a little, then I gave the stool a little whirl to bring it up to my height and when he saw that he stopped walking because that gave him an idea that maybe I knew what I was doing. Then I sat down and I started on the number and I played it all the way through, and then I sang the words along with it and when I stopped all the girls started talking and coming up to me and I said, what would you like me to play for you now? I was ready for anything they might ask for and one of them asked for a ragtime number, which was what I was hoping for, and when I got through with it there was so much noise you couldn't have heard a train if it had come driving through the room. And I looked around and Bill was putting his hat on and getting it very straight on his head. He had one of those little derby hats and he was getting it set just so. I thought he was just going to walk out of there and leave me sitting there at the piano, but I saw him turn around and wave with his hand and I saw the crowd kind of give way and there was Skinny Walter coming through towards me. Now the girls saw what was going to happen and they got in the way but Skinny Walter just stretched out those big arms of his and pushed them out of the way like they were leaves on the trees. One or two of them kept hanging on to him, because they knew he never would do anything to a woman, but I just kept sitting there. I didn't have any place to run to and I couldn't fight him. All I had was the fingers I used to play the piano with and the fingers I used to play pool with and I wasn't going to try using them on a man like that.

I didn't even want to look up, but when you have somebody standing right there that wants to beat your ass you better look at him to see what he's doing so I looked up and he said, so you're some smart kid. I said, all I wanted to do was play the piano a little. No, he said, you wanted to hustle this man here. And he pointed over to Bill, who was leaning against the bar with his hat still on. When you come in here you give me some story about a pawn ticket and then I see you hanging around looking up the girls' dresses and then you sit down and try to make a monkey out of Bill here. I was beginning to get frightened because people were getting quiet and moving back out of the way like they do when there's a fight coming. So I said to him I wasn't trying to make a monkey out of anybody. Of course I could have said Bill didn't need any help in that line because he was making a monkey out of himself every time he touched the piano, but I decided that with Skinny Walter standing over me like that I would do better to show my respects. I said to him that I did a little singing and a little playing and I only sat down at the stool because some of his customers had expressed their interest in hearing a number that Bill hadn't had a chance to rehearse and I was only interested in giving them a little entertainment.

So Skinny Walter looked over at Bill and he said, he's just a kid. So it was up to Bill and all he had to do to get me thrown out of there was say to Skinny Walter that I was trying to hustle him. I could see him standing there studying me and the whole place was getting quieter and quieter because they knew something was going on. Now I had my fancy clothes on and all, but I didn't look like more than a kid and he'd heard me play and he knew I was better than he was. It didn't make no difference to Skinny Walter and he was standing there waiting for Bill to say something, and if Bill said run him out of here he was going to whip my ass. But I could see Bill's face working and I could see the girls looking at him and finally Bill turned around to the bar and he kind of sighed because he knew I could play and he said boy, you know any opera numbers and everybody turned to me and I was getting nervous but I had a number that was very popular in New Orleans, and that number was the Miserere from Il Trovatore and I called out the name in kind of a shaky voice and I started playing it in my style.

Well I could hear the girls start to shout and people were stamping on the floor and out of the corner of my eye I could see Bill, and after I had played a couple of choruses I saw him kind of shake

his head and he shrugged his shoulders and Skinny
Walter turned around and went back to the door. So
I was alright and Bill let me stay there until I was
ready to move on. But that place was rough. There
wasn't any place in Pensacola that was rougher than
Boodie's. So like I said, when we got started in to
talking the Jungle Inn here maybe isn't so high-class,
but it isn't one of the places where anything goes. Of
course I had a little trouble here a while back with
one of those so-called tough boys and he gave me a
little cutting, but nobody's going to bother a
customer. You can come here anytime and nothing's
going to happen to you. In a place like Boodie's you
better know who was standing behind you because in
a place like that anything could happen.

Now you would think that what had happened would
cause Bill to quit, but he kept coming to the place
every night and he let me teach him a few things
about chords and so forth and so on. Of course that
wasn't hard for me to do because that man knew no
doubt less about the piano than any musician I ever
met. Now you wonder why he let me get away with
my hustling. Sometimes I wonder myself. He could
have been real tough with me and he could have told
Skinny Walter to get this kid out of here, but he
didn't. In my early days the same thing had happened
once to me. In New Orleans when I just had got

23

started in the sporting houses and I had taken a little job playing, a fellow came in and I knew who he was. His name was Alfred Wilson and later on he took the first prize at the St. Louis Exposition in 1904. I got so I could take him later on, but then I was just a beginner and he did the same thing to me that I did to Bill. He asked me to play some number so he could sing and people asked him to sing it and I got up off the stool and let him have it because I knew who he was and I knew he could play. I know for myself I did it because I was proud of being a piano player. I suppose that was going through Bill's mind when I did it to him. Everyone of us was proud of what we could play, but if somebody could do better we let him. We'd get our own chance later on.

The fact of the matter is we didn't have so many things that the white people would let us do, so we took them very seriously. Very seriously. So if somebody could play better, then that was a step up for all of us. In a manner of speaking it made us all look better. Of course if somebody did catch us with some new numbers you can be damn sure we tried to catch him right back with some new numbers of our own, and if he had some lick that we didn't know we'd go through the neighborhood like a dog after his lady until we'd find a piano and we would work out that lick for ourselves. Then we would hunt him down and come right back at him with his own lick, and he would have to come up with something new to stay ahead of the rest of us.

Of course, when you think about it you have to ask yourself what we were doing in such a low environment as places like Boodie's. Most of the time you didn't get any regular pay, just what you could make out of the kitty and if there was a fight and somebody got shot the place would close down and you wouldn't have a job until it opened up again. I hate to say it, but the truth is we didn't have anyplace that was any better. There was the shows and all — the minstrels and the medicine shows, but you had to smear your face up with burnt cork and you had to paint your lips all big and fat like you were wearing some kind of funny mask and you had to carry on with all that laughing and that stuff like "gwine" and all those kind of nigger words you had to say. But where we were playing, in those honky tonks, nobody was listening to hear if we were using all those words we were supposed to be using. I don't mean to say nothing against anybody. I'm not the kind of person that lets his mouth get on ahead of him, but for a certain class of white people there wasn't no way you could be your own self around them. You always had to keep looking down when you talked to them and you had to use all kind of funny words 'cause that's the way they thought colored people should act like. Of course when you go out on the road you do what the public expects of you, and many's the time I did that myself, all that bowing your head and using those words, standing in the middle of the street and hoping the fellow that was standing there in front of you would just let you get past. You'd want to laugh right up at him, right there to his face, but at the same time you knew it wasn't wise to get him all worked up.

That's why we had our own clubs and our own two-bit honky tonks where they had all kind of rough people. When you come inside the door you wasn't going to have no white person tell you what you should be doing and so on and so forth. Of course you had to be careful of some of those colored boys and sometimes you'd have to hang your head when they talked too, but you didn't have to act like no damned nigger. I never say anything unless it comes from the real facts and that's the truth of the matter. Those places were low. Some of them were so low you'd have to crawl on your belly just to come in through the door. But they were our own places and nobody could bother us unless they had some kind of raid and they got a truck or a wagon and they branged in the whole police force. Some of those places you'd have to bring in the army to get inside them if the man at the door didn't like your face.

Now the white people had their own places and they didn't want us to get too close anyway, so if we had our own little clubs to go to then they kind of let it be. But in them little bitty towns in the country where there'd be just the store and maybe a garage and a post office the white man who owned the one club around, he'd divide the place down the middle and he'd have half of it set up for white and half of it for colored. I've seen these places myself in some of the towns strung up along the Mississippi River out of New Orleans. You take your car or your wagon and they have those curvy little roads that run right alongside the levee and you ride out along there and if you feel yourself getting thirsty which would only be natural with the sun burning down on you, then of course you look around for someplace to get you a little drink. Now this building would be the only place around there. Old run-down kind of places with board sides and if somebody had ever thought of putting a coat of paint on them they'd given up the thought as a bad idea. Then they'd have two separate entrances, with a door in the front for white and a door in the back for colored. They even had two different places to park your car, although cars came after the time I'm telling you about.

Inside the place there'd be a partition running right down the middle of the room and there'd be two bars, one on either side of the partition and they'd have tables and chairs and so forth and maybe at one end they'd have a little platform where one of those country string bands with a violin and a guitar could entertain. Many's the time when I traveled out to those places when I was still a kid and I waited for the person who had brought me to hurry up with his beer, and I could see past the partition into the white side. Now where we were sitting, the colored, everything was all busted up and raggedy. The chairs didn't have backs to them and the tables had propped-up legs that were all out of balance. If the place had electricity there'd be a couple of little bulbs hanging down from the wire on the colored side, and if you were playing cards you had to hold your hand up to the lamp to see if you had an ace of spades or an ace of hearts. I'm telling you, those places were bad. And I'd be standing there trying not to be noticed and I could see into the white side and it was all nice and there was pictures on the wall and the spittoons were all shined up.

Now if a fellow was running this kind of an establishment he would be very angry if a Negro tried to get something going which would be in competition with him. So the Negro fellow would have to get himself a shack out on the edge of town. I'm telling you some of those colored honky tonks I frequented in those days were so far out in the country you'd have to pack a sandwich so you wouldn't die of hunger before you got there. The fact of the matter is, in a place like that the music wasn't so good most times on account of the piano. You hear people talking about this and that battle of music, but a lot of times when I'd go into one of those low-class kind of places the only battle I'd get into would be with the piano. There was some which it would have been better to take to the old folks' home, I tell you. If there was anything on the piano that still was working it was only because the fellow who'd been playing it the night before hadn't known about it. Now I was considered to be the best around for the left hand even in those days, and if the piano wasn't working good I'd have to feel my way around to see what I could do with it.

I remember one time a little gal asked me to come play at this club she was running, and since I had it in my mind to get next to her I told her I'd come around that evening and when I come into the place there was this little piano all painted white over by the bar. I came in, you know, like a real tickler, as piano players were called in those days, in my hundred dollar suit of clothes and the latest style in shoes and I had a brand new overcoat with a very flashy lining, and when I'd come into a place I'd take off this coat very carefully, like it was made out of solid gold, and I'd fold back the coat so everybody could get a look at the lining. Then I'd lay the coat down along the top of the piano, being very careful with the way it was folded, and then I would take out a silk handkerchief which I always had in my pocket just for such occasions and I would dust off the piano stool so as not to get my trousers soiled. Then I'd be ready to sit down and play.

So I did all this and I pulled back the sleeves on my coat to let everyone see my cufflinks and I looked around to see if the lady was watching me and she gave me a smile so I put my fingers on the keys to start one of my specialty numbers and I played some notes with my left hand and there was nothing there. Not a note. Of course I felt just like the fool that runs after a train and gets there just when it gets going too fast and everybody leaning out of the window starts laughing at him. That little piano looked so shiny and new with that white paint, but everything was gone inside it where you play with the left hand. I did some fast thinking and before anybody could see what had happened I started making some little chords up in the top of the piano where the keys worked and I began singing some kind of dirty song, but playing up high like that I had to put my voice way up to reach the notes and I could see with my clothes and the tinkly little chords I was making and the high voice I was singing that people would misunderstand me so there was nothing for me to do but get out of the place. I never did see that lady again but there was many a time I thought of going back to her place and telling her what I thought of her little queer piano.

It was very often in those days that you would come into one of those clubs and the only music

29

they had was string bands. It was because of those bad pianos. If a fellow come in with a guitar or a violin that was his own he had to keep it ready to play. I was just a little boy in New Orleans, but when I went around to listen in to the door of the clubs I'd hear piano players sometimes or maybe a little band, but mostly I'd hear somebody with a guitar or a mandolin. That was some beautiful music those boys could make. You don't hear any more of it now. All the numbers they played had plenty melody and beautiful rhythm. Sometimes I'd go walking down in the French Quarter around those big apartments around Jackson Square and at night you'd hear the fellows serenading and they always had guitars with them. I mean, they weren't serenading because they wanted some lady to hear them. These was colored boys out to make a little money and they'd stand under the balconies along the square singing songs up to the people that lived there and the people would throw them down money. They'd do their serenading in the evenings and let me tell you it was beautiful to hear them singing in the quiet there with maybe some horses going by or one of the steamboats along the river. They didn't sing any blues. The blues came later. What they sang was songs like "After The Ball" and "My Gal Sal" and that type of number. I did a little of it myself. I started on the guitar and I learned some songs, but it was so hard for a kid to get in on it so that's when I devoted myself to the piano.

People nowadays hear so much about jazz that they don't know what New Orleans was really like back in those days. We had all kinds of music. We had your low class barrel house kind of honky tonk music and we had your operas and symphonies and all those classical numbers like "Poet and Peasant" which was very popular. There was no doubt more different kinds of music than you could find anywhere on the face of the globe.

Now the reason for that was the Creole people. Take my own family. They was Frenchmens from way back and they had all kinds of music. We were living Uptown at that time but Downtown was where the Creole people lived, right off of South Rampart Street. When I was very young these people had all the privileges of white people although they was what you would call mixed blood. That is they had people in their background from both sides of the tracks. The French people didn't worry so much about that and they let these families grow up alongside them and they learned the French language and all that music. Of course I was accepted by these people because of my own family and I would go down to this part of New Orleans on Sunday afternoons when they would go calling as they called it, and they would go from one house to another wearing their best clothes. They had so many beautiful dressers, men and women both, and the women would be in a long gown, the kind that came right down to the street and they would have on hats with very broad brims and trimmed with all kind of feathers. And of course, once they'd get to somebody's house they would have maybe coffee or tea and after they had talked for a little somebody would play a little music.

The music they played wasn't jazz, any more than the songs those boys were singing around Jackson Square were blues songs. This was a very cultured class of people and they had only the finest type of music, overtures and symphonies and other numbers of that type. I myself studied music for a short time with Professor Henry Nickerson who had undertaken to teach me the violin. In those days they still had their French Opera and some of the finest musicians in the country were the Creole gentlemen playing in the orchestra. Among the professors of music there was Professor Anthony Page and Professor Charles Deverges and Professor Luis Tio who was together with Professor Doublet in the little orchestra which they managed together. They had all kinds of music and practically every Friday night there was what they called a "Calico Ball", which took the name from the ladies' dresses. Nothing but high class music and they didn't do any of that low kind of dancing, the slow drags and that type of number. When you came to one of those Creole dances you did the quadrille and the two step and the mazurka and of course so many lovely waltzes.

Sometimes when I'm talking to somebody about New Orleans and about those old days that fellow will say to me, hold on, if you got everything so good down there, what are you doing here? Something in that line and I can see he's a little jealous on account of me being from there. But this is something I have to explain about. You might have noticed when I speak about the places I have been and traveled you don't hear me talking about Mississippi or Alabama or Georgia or any place in those parts of the South. In my younger days, before I knew what I was doing, I stayed around those kind of places, but when I came to know more about what was going on I didn't go back. And that was on account of the way they treated Negroes. It didn't make any difference if your skin was light or dark, everywhere you were treated just the same. Which means you were treated very poor. Now I hate to say something like this, but in New Orleans the white people had the same feelings. When I was very small the Creole people had their own way of living and they didn't have to put up with the same things the real black people did, but when I was somewhere around ten years old the white people passed a law taking all that away from the Creoles and making them just like dark complexioned people when it came to riding in the back part of the street cars or taking jobs or going into their own businesses. Now we could have learned how to do something about that, but then when I was a little bit older another thing happened and that made every Negro in New Orleans know that he couldn't expect anything from the white people. I was just fourteen years old, and that's a time in your life when anything that happens to you goes very deep. What it was that happened can be said in one man's name, and it's a name that struck fear into the heart of every white person in New Orleans. That name was Robert Charles.

Now, many people have asked me about Robert Charles and I have gave them many different stories about what happened in New Orleans at that time. The reason I gave out so many stories was that you have to be careful with that name today. There are people who will become angry with you just for saying Robert Charles' name. You have heard me tell many stories and I know you don't carry things further, so I can tell you what I know to be the truth about this man, and I am in a position to know because I lived in the same neighborhood as Robert Charles and I used to see him on the street when he was going around with those newspapers. I believe if it had not been for what happened in New Orleans at that time I might still be living there today, and I know there was many other boys feeling just the same way. It showed us what the people of New Orleans really were like, and we never could forget it. Suppose you had came down to Canal Street on Mardi Gras Day, which I had done many a time as a small boy, and at the same minute everybody out on the street took off their masks. Well, that's what happened to us. All the masks came off and New Orleans never was the same.

Before I tell you the story of Robert Charles I have to tell you the name of another man. It was a name that people didn't remember so well except just at that time. But all the boys around New Orleans knew his name and I don't suppose there was a colored person in the South who couldn't tell you about what happened. That man's name was Sam Holt. The troubles with Robert Charles were in the summer, and I know the year because I don't suppose I'll ever forget it. The year was 1900. Now the year before, something happened to this man named Sam Holt and there was people who said that it was that thing that led to what happened after. Sam Holt was a colored gentleman who got into trouble in Georgia, somewhere outside of Atlanta. The word went out among the white people that Sam Holt had raped a white woman. Now nobody ever knew if it was the truth, but before you could get the story straight there had sprung up a mob which went out and captured this man. Of course, if you were a Negro you knew what would come next, but this time that mob decided they would do it in a very artistic fashion. They weren't in any hurry, and they didn't figure Sam Holt would be going anywhere.

So they tortured him for a time, and they all seemed to be enjoying it so much the railroad put on special trains out from Atlanta so people could come watch, and since it was a Sunday thousands of people thought they would come out, and women and children made the journey, whole families went along to see what they were doing to this man. After a while there wasn't much use in torturing him any more so they hung him up over a fire and began burning him while he still was alive. Finally Sam Holt died but all these people had came out to see everything. So they took him out of the fire before he was all burned up and they took out his heart and his liver and they cut little slices off them and sold them to anybody who wanted them for a souvenir. There was one fellow who took his slice of the heart on the train with him back to Atlanta with the purpose of presenting it to the Governor of Georgia. You may not believe this happened, but we didn't just hear some story about it from some country fellow who got it all twisted around. This was in the newspapers for everybody to read, and one of the people who read it was Robert Charles.

There were many stories about how the trouble

with Robert Charles started. I heard people say one thing or another thing. One story which seemed to be very popular was that Robert was having trouble with his wife which caused her to call for the police, and when they came to arrest him they wouldn't let him go back into the house for his hat and he grew angry and he broke loose and began to fire his pistol at the police. But what some people said afterwards, when they began to see everything a little better, was that Robert wasn't doing anything, he just was sitting out on the street at night with the fellow that rented a room with him. He had gone out to see his sister, but she wasn't home and they had taken a seat where they shouldn't have to wait for her. Three policemen came up to them and they asked questions about what their business was and Robert stood up which frightened the police since he was a large man and one policeman grabbed him and started hitting him on the head with his billy club. But Robert was too big for him and when they got out into the middle of the street Robert broke loose. Seeing that he couldn't do anything trying to fight with Robert the policeman took out his pistol and shot him in the leg and Robert took out his own pistol, which he always had in his coat pocket, and he shot the policeman and ran off down the street leaving a trail of blood behind him.

Now if that had been all there was to it then the trouble never would have started, except for the fact it was a time when you couldn't read a newspaper without reading all kinds of things about how Negroes — of course they didn't call them that — hated all white people and they were only waiting their chance to cause trouble. The other two

NEGRO KILLS BLUECOATS AND ESCAPES

Shoots Down Captain John T. Day and Patrolman Peter J. Lamb.

MURDERER, CURSING HIS VICTIMS, FIRES INTO THEIR LIFELESS FORMS.

Populace Inflamed, and Armed Mobs Throng the Streets—Mayor Capdevielle offers $250 Reward for Murderer's Capture, "Dead or Alive"—Gov. Heard Follows With Additional Offer of $250 Reward.

Robert Charles

++++++++++ ++++++++++

ROBERT CHARLES, MURDERER.

Brown skinned negro.

Age thirty.

Height about six feet.

Weight about 180 pounds.

Hair slightly kinky, closely cropped.

Moustache long, black and straight.

Two upper front teeth decayed and discolored.

Eyes small and beady.

Slight limp in left foot.

Fond of talking about race wrongs and Liberia emigration project.

Drinks, but not to excess.

Supposed to be a cocaine user.

++++++++++ ++++++++++

Between 2:30 and 5 o'clock yesterday morning Police Captain John T. Day and Patrolman Peter J. Lamb were shot dead by Robert Charles, the negro desperado who seriously wounded Officer August T. Mora earlier in the night.

The scene of the double murder was a gloomy little alley, lying behind a closed door on Fourth street, between Saratoga and South Rampart. It led past a squalid barracks, with five doors opening into as many rooms, used as lodgings in the night.

whistle summoning Patrolmen August T. Mora and Paul Cantrelle, and the three proceeded to the doorstep and attempted to place the negroes under arrest.

The pair resisted, drew pistols and an indiscriminate street duel ensued, the officers firing from the roadway and the negroes from the sidewalk. Mora fell at the first exchange, hit hard in the left thigh and wounded slightly in both hands. Charles ran toward Sixth street, bleeding from a wound, and after emptying his pistol disappeared in the darkness. Pearson stood his ground and fired two shots, when his revolver stuck and he surrendered.

That was the beginning of the night's tragic work. Charles was seen going up Sixth street, holding his abdomen as if

++++++++++ ++++++++++

A negro, answering in near-

Leaving the Pitkin woman's house they walked out to the corner of Sixth and Dryades streets, where they loafed around, supposedly waiting for the two women, for about half an hour. Pierson then suggested that they had better move as the police would think that they were up to mischief, and he did not care to be ordered away. Charles then suggested that they move up to the box steps in the middle of the block and sit down there and wait until the women should arrive. As near as he could remember this was about 10:15 o'clock. They had noticed the three women who complained about their loitering. They had not been seated on the steps more than five minutes when the sergeant and two other officers came up and asked them what they were doing there. He had replied that they were waiting for two women who were coming from the depot. Charles made no reply, but got up and began "edging off."

One of the officers called to him, "Come back here!" and at the same time the sergeant placed his pistol to Pierson's face and commanded him not to move.

He threw up his hands instantly and said to the policeman, "You don't need to shoot me, officer. I ain't done nothin' to be shot or 'rested for, an' I ain't goin' to run."

Charles had started to run away in the

policeman still had the fellow who rented a room with Robert, and of course they finally got him to say who he was and where he lived and when he told them they got some more policemen and took out after Robert. Robert had ran back to his room ahead of them. He knew that having shot a policeman he was a dead man and he was determined that a mob would never get their hands on him. So he went back to his room to get his Winchester repeating rifle. The policemen got to the front of the house before he was able to get away and he waited inside the door for them. When the first policeman came into sight, which was the Captain of the New Orleans police, Robert raised his rifle and shot him through the heart. He then took aim again with his rifle and killed the second policeman with one shot. When they saw that the Captain had been killed the other policemen ran away and Robert was able to make his escape.

All of this had taken place on Tuesday morning, and when the police and the newspaper reporters went into Robert's room they found these papers he had been giving out telling Negroes the only chance they had was to get out and go back to Africa. He had taken up with this after hearing about Sam Holt in Georgia. Now, to the white people this meant Robert was trying to start a revolution by the Negroes in New Orleans and when he stood up to the police and shot his rifle at them they decided the revolution had already started. Of course the young people like myself heard about what was happening right away and I was still living at home at that time, so as soon as I got the news I came back and stayed inside. But that night the mobs started through the streets, running up and down St. Charles Avenue looking for any colored person they could find. It didn't matter if it was a man or a woman or if that person was old or young. The street cars were still running up and down St. Charles Avenue and there were people coming back from their work or their errands and so forth and so on, and the gangs stopped the street cars and took any colored people off them that they could find and they commenced beating them.

All night it went on and the next day everywhere you could look there were white men to be seen carrying rifles and shotguns and every kind of pistols. I and my two sisters stayed hid the entire time, but we didn't know at any moment if those fellows would break in the door and pull us out into the street with them. That same night, which was a Wednesday, the mob was out again and they went through the streets of Storyville looking for any sign of Negroes, and the whores from the houses came out and stood on the steps and cheered for those white men. One of the orchestras that was playing in the district, Henry Peyton's bunch at the 25, which was at the corner of Iberville and Franklin, they didn't think they would get into any trouble, but when they heard the shooting they understood they would have to run for it and they just got out before the people came after them. They hid all night in a house with the door barred.

It wasn't until Friday afternoon that the police found out where Robert Charles was hiding and by this time Negroes were lying in the hospitals and Negroes were lying in the morgue. A great number had been killed and for everyone killed fifty had been beaten. For many days after I saw men and women with their arms or their heads covered in bandages and I saw the houses which had a wreath placed on the door. Of course we heard the sounds of the guns going off when the police found the house Robert was hiding in. My sisters and I ran to the windows, but so many white people were running to get there we pulled down so nobody would see us. It sounded like it was a battle, with all kinds of guns going off. It was later determined that Robert had a machine for making his own bullets, and when they discovered him he was ready for them. He had decided he would not be taken alive and he would kill as many white people as he was able before the breath left his body. Each time he would pull the trigger on his Winchester a man would go down. With his first two bullets two policemen fell dead and when the priest came to give the sacrament he fired again and a man standing beside the priest was the next to die. When at last a bullet ended Robert Charles' life, the ground was covered with men wounded and dying. Then when he was dead they dragged his body out into the street and they shot it full of bullets and people kicked at it and hit it with sticks, and then they arrested everybody who had been living in the house where he was hiding and accused them of murder. My grandmother went out and got us some groceries the next day, but it wasn't until Sunday morning that we dared to show ourselves on the street and then it was only due to the necessity of attending Mass.

Those were bad times, I'm telling you. If you haven't lived through an experience of that nature then you are still a beginner in the human race. Of course after a couple of months everybody tried to act like nothing had ever happened, but if you had been there in that week you would always have it inside your mind everytime you would get angry at some of the things which were done to you. The fact of the matter was the white people did things their own way in New Orleans, just like they are still everywhere today. I think they had the idea that if they weren't chasing us along the streets they were doing all that the Lord required of them along the line of equality. It wasn't only the dark class of people which had just came in from the country, they treated us the same way and I was lighter than some of those fellows who were out on the streets with their guns looking for Robert Charles.

The fact of the matter is they just wanted us out of the way. They didn't want us to have any jobs, not even the little jobs doing street cleaning and washing windows and carrying sacks of corn meal and so forth and so on, which is all most of the dark complexion kind of people could do anyway. They didn't want us to have jobs or money or buy property. They kept telling each other they were trying to keep us from getting at their white women, but we had so many pretty women of our own we weren't any of us thinking about looking in another direction. But the truth is, in the music line it didn't work out the way they had in mind. If they had let everything be open, all the clubs and the restaurants and let everybody come into the orchestras, and if they had let us come into the schools and learn the same things they did, I don't know if we would have something called jazz music today. I don't know if there would be a colored man in America doing anything different from what a white man does. But they shut us out so we had to come up with something on our own, and now everywhere in the world it's our music and our rhythm and our compositions which have came out on top, so in the end it all came right back on them.

Of course I wasn't thinking any of these things when I was a kid. I was just looking for a way to get a little bit ahead and where you started was in the honky tonks, and if you had a talent and you could find somebody to teach you a little something you could come into the sporting houses which was where the real money was to be made. That was where we all strived to be. Now when I look back on it I know that wasn't a place for a little boy to hang out. The women there were selling themselves and they had all kind of pimps and sporting men to help them, and all around the women there were men selling bad liquor and cocaine and the gambling games in the saloons were so crooked even the tops of the tables weren't on the level. But that was the only place I could go if I wanted to get a good suit of clothes and a gold watch chain and a pair of shoes made out of shiny leather.

My being a piano player was not appreciated by my family, which was my grandmother and my sisters after my father and mother had passed away, and this was the cause of much unhappiness to me, since my grandmother was of the old type of Creole family which would not stand for anything in the line of sporting houses or gambling. When my grandmother learned of my being a piano player and hanging around in the district, she said she would not have me setting a bad example for my sisters and I would have to leave. So I was forced to go out on my own when I was still too young even to know how to get out of bed without somebody nudging my shoulder. This caused me to be in the district more than ever before, though first I went off to Biloxi and stayed a little time with my godmother to get my feet on the ground, and there I commenced my traveling. But once I started working all the time in the houses there always was somebody to talk to, which could have been the start of the way I talk today. You wouldn't think that you could talk to the girls in the sporting houses. A lot of them was very low class, although they no doubt were very pretty and knew how to get a man interested in what it was they were selling, and out on the street there were all kinds of women working who were even lower class. But they all were doing just the same as we were. They were just trying to get along as best they could.

I started hanging around there when I was very small, just a little bitty kid. In the afternoons before the business really got started they'd let us boys hang around and they'd tell us all kind of jokes and let us have a sandwich or a beer. Of course at the age I was then I wasn't interested in anything else. I'm telling you they had girls that came from every part of the United States and girls that came from all the different countries in the world, and some of them couldn't talk English, so the ladies that ran the houses said they were Russian princesses or French countesses or something like that. When we'd get smart and start in to sass them they'd get a little salty with us and say we were nothing but niggers, but we'd run off a little so they couldn't catch us and we'd come back at them that they weren't nothing but whores and sometimes they'd throw something at us and there was one girl who picked up her skirt and came running after us right down the street.

I remember something happening one time with a girl I'd gotten kind of used to seeing in one of the places. She couldn't have been much more than fourteen or fifteen and she still was all pretty and she would laugh when I did kind of crazy stunts to amuse her. One day she got a little hasty with me and I ran off a little like I was used to and I turned around and I pulled out the suspenders on the little boy's short trousers I was wearing and I told her she wasn't nothing but a whore and she wasn't going to be nothing but a whore and she stood there looking at me and her mouth got real big and she started crying. I never did go back to that house to see her again.

So after all the places I have been and seen and what I have been through I don't let myself get all worried about someplace like The Jungle Inn. I have played in so many that were so much worser. Washington's not a bad little town and we've had some lovely crowds which have came down to hear me play piano and the public had gave me the idea that they like to hear me sing, even if my voice is kind of rough for the type of songs they have today, so I give them those kind of numbers. In fact I give them any kind of numbers they want to hear. I try to make sure the place is cleaned up before we start the show and I always select the girls that come to work here so we don't have somebody stealing a little on the drinks and at the same time she's doing a little business of her own on the side. With my music the place doesn't need to be selling anything else.

Of course the club never closes down while we still have somebody that's spending money and there's a party down at the end of the bar good for another hour's drinking. As you may have noticed I don't take more than two or three drinks myself as it doesn't sit so well with my stomach, but I have to say I have no doubt spent the best part of my life in bar rooms and honky tonks, and it seems very natural to sit down at a table and pass a little time talking and drinking as the club gets ready to close. The fact of the matter is maybe I could have made more out of my life if I had devoted more time to other interests. I could have been very popular in many other lines of work, but I thought of myself first and foremost as a piano player and as an entertainer. Of course there was plenty money in those old days. That's a fact. Plenty money. With all those sporting houses and all those boys who was big spenders wanting to show off for their girls by giving a big tip to the piano player. If I had a day where I made seventy or a hundred dollars I thought that day didn't amount to anything at all. Today if I make five or ten dollars I think that's a big day. That goes to show you the difference with the times we have today.

In those days I wouldn't work in a place like this one. I was very particular about the places where I come to work. I was telling you about that club over in Pensacola, that honky tonk called Boodie's. I was just a kid then. Nothing much more than a boy, and when I moved on from there I had some money in my pocket so I could get me a new suit of clothes that didn't have that oyster smell and by that means I could get myself inside the better class of night clubs and honky tonks and sporting houses and so forth and so on. I came back to New Orleans and every door was open to me. I had got myself a $100 suit of clothes when I came to town, I remember it was 1905, and when I had those new clothes the girls would stand outside on the steps of the houses waiting for me to pass their doors.

Many of the other piano players in town seem to have accepted me as superior so I could go into a sporting house and take over that man's job for as long as I wanted to stay, and I always was sure to have some new kind of numbers to play when I come back into town. New Orleans wasn't a place where they'd let you rest. There was always boys looking for a battle of music and that was where the new numbers come in. If you had a new number and they couldn't cut it then you were considered to be the winner and there would be all kinds of drinks and a party right there on the spot.

I don't think there was anywhere on the globe with sporting houses to match up with what they had set up there in New Orleans. Genuine crystal chandeliers imported from Europe. Curtains made from pure silk and the finest carpets. If you had a man come in from Panama then they would call to the waiter who could talk to the man in Spanish. If they had Frenchmens they would go upstairs to find the girls who could talk to them in French. The same with men from Germany or anyplace in the world. They always could find something for them. I will tell a story on myself about a trick I and another fellow played on a rich man we met on the street. I shouldn't tell it, but those were different times and when you're young you're a little careless about things you do. This other fellow and I had just gotten up and we were taking a little walk down in the French Quarter when we had finished our breakfasts, and of course we had been up all the night before because he worked in the sporting house like I did, so it was the middle of the afternoon and we just were starting in on the day. We had on our finest clothes because if you were out at that time you didn't want to give anybody the impression that you were working. If you came down the street and you had on a new suit of clothes and you had a necktie and a clean shirt people would know you were just out walking and they would get a different idea about you.

So we were coming down Dauphine Street, I suppose it must have been somewhere around Orleans Street where that lovely old building stood on the corner, and we were standing there in the

47

shade under the balcony and a Frenchman comes down the street. We didn't know he was French until he opened his mouth but we could see by the way he was looking at everything that he didn't know where he was. Anyway he came up to us and he started talking to us in French about how he was looking for something. I had came from a long line of Frenchmen so I answered him back the same way. That seemed to surprise him, but he was so glad to talk that he started talking even faster. He was supposed to go to a church meeting. He was going to meet with a Father who was going to give him some sort of a letter to take back to Paris. I never did get that part of it. But he went on talking and his face was all red from the sun and he was in a very nice suit of clothes, but he was fanning himself with a lace handkerchief and he had on shoes with funny kind of spats, so we started to think of some way to have a little fun. My friend whispered something in my ear and I told the man in my own French that we would take him to the Father's residence and we'd send somebody ahead to tell the Father he was coming. Now what we done was to tell a boy on the street to go back to the house where we were working.

Now, the man didn't know where the boy was running to. We had gave him a nickel to go into the house and tell one of the girls there what we wanted her to do, then we come walking along together. We never could have done it if those houses weren't so elegant and it was the afternoon so there wasn't anybody out on the sidewalk to give it away. We got to the house and it was just down the street from a church and we said to the man that this was the residence and he should come in with us and we'd

show him where to find the Father and so forth and
so on. Of course we could see the boy from the
window waving to us to tell us everything was all set
up like we wanted it. We got the man in the front
parlor and he looked around at everything and he was
very impressed. It was all very elegant, you
understand. There was nothing that was cheap about
it. He looked at the curtains and the furnishings. It
was all very swell. With all the chairs and the little
tables you could see it was supposed to be for a
number of people, but he thought it was just where
people waited when they wanted to see the Father
and he stood there fanning himself with his
handkerchief and looking very pleased to see where
he was. Then we took him to the sliding door that led
into the second parlor and we opened up the door
and let him go in by himself.

What we told the boy was to run upstairs and get
this girl we knew and then she was supposed to come
down into the back room and wait on the divan that
was just across from the door. Then the minute this
man walked in she was supposed to pull up her dress
and open up her legs and give this man the surprise of
his life. Of course they didn't wear anything under
the dresses there in the house so he was going to get
something he didn't expect at all. So we stood to one
side and let him go in and we could hear something
swishing and he let out a noise like somebody had
stuck him in the ass with a poker, and he came
running out of there and fell down over a chair and
he saw us standing there and we were trying not to
fall down from laughing and he said to me in that
French of his, that wasn't the Father. And I answered
him back, did you get a look at his face? And the girl

49

started to come out into the room and she was laughing as hard as we were and she started to pull up her dress again and that fellow took on out of there like the place was going to burn up on him if he didn't get away, and we started laughing so hard we all fell down right where we were standing and we'd tell each other about the look on his face and we'd start laughing again and it was an hour before we could stand up on our two feet and we gave the girl a dollar for her part in it and she went away very content.

Those were the days, I'm telling you. Of course it seems to me that the life I was living in those days was as different from things today as it would be if I had been living in another part of the globe, and no doubt everybody thinks the same way when they come to look back, but the fact of the matter is, times were different then. I can remember traveling on wagons and on little bitty carts pulled by horses and mules and the trains those days was so smoky I'm telling you you'd get the collar of your shirt dirty just climbing up the steps into the car. Of course you're younger than I am and no doubt you are going to see changes just as I have seen so many changes, though I don't believe there will ever again be so many changes as I have seen in my travels which have taken me into every part of this country.

I don't suppose in my travels there has been a state or a city that I have not appeared in with a show or played the piano in a night club or a honky tonk. People ask me sometime, Jelly, why did you do all that traveling? And I tell them I wanted to let people see me. There was no way for people to know of my abilities unless they could see me in person and if I were to become known I didn't have a choice except to go on the road. Of course, some fellows they don't feel that way. They have some little thing going for them and they're content to stay with that. But I taken to myself the notion that I could be more popular. I believed that people throughout the nation should have the opportunity to hear what I could do. I know for a fact I'm not alone in taking that to be my course of action for I have met so many fellows who were out traveling the same as I was. Sometimes they'd be traveling in a big car and sometimes they'd be riding the rods but they would always be on the move. Sometimes we'd hook up together for a while so we could be partners since we all were looking for the same thing. The fact of the matter is I think most everybody you meet has the same idea except they don't have the nerve enough to go do it. Everybody wants to be known in this life and he wants people to recognize his abilities but sometimes he doesn't know how to go about it. I hate to say a thing like this, but I was the kind of person that had this knowledge and now there are people everywhere I go who know my name and they know what I can do.

Now, if I had been a different kind of a person I had all kinds of opportunities right where I was. If I had stayed on in New Orleans I could have had plenty money and any girls I wanted. I was well known in the district and I could walk into any one of those sporting houses and the man sitting on the piano stool would get up and give me his place. Before the night was through I'd have big money from the tips people gave me for playing the numbers they requested, and if they had any specialty numbers where they wanted a little music from out of sight while the girls danced without their clothes on for private parties, I could pull a curtain in front of the piano and I could play for all that kind of stuff. It was very often that the boys, to get themselves recognized as a real piano player, would give themselves alias names and the name I was known by was Winding Ball and that's what the girls called me. I'd go down Basin Street and I'd hear them calling out the window to me, Winding Ball, Winding Ball. But I didn't think New Orleans was big enough for me. You might say that's the story of my life. I was always looking for someplace that was big enough for me and I'm still looking today.

Now, in those times there was one place that I seemed to have a yen to go back to for a number of reasons and that place was Mexico. You ask me, why Mexico, and I'll tell you. I wasn't the only fellow that went down to Mexico in those days. You see, in Mexico there wasn't any trouble on account of your color. They didn't have much in the way of big night clubs and if you did make a name for yourself down there it didn't carry no further than the border, but you could go to Mexico and be accepted. You can say all you want about how a man has to make his way as best he can and not let anybody stand in his way, but in those days it seemed like all the ways were blocked for the colored people. Of course I maybe shouldn't say things like this, but you and I are sitting here drinking and I know you understand the things I'm telling you. In those days I would have had too much sense to ever tell these things to another person, white or colored, for fear of what might happen to me. The fact of the matter is nobody ever will understand what America was like in those days unless they keep in their minds the way the Negro was kept down. It's something that I don't believe will ever be forgotten, but even today there's people who don't want to hear about what it was like. You can read in all kind of books about how everything is just fine, but it's the white people who are writing the books for each other and if they asked a Negro to give his side of it then the books no doubt would have a different story in them.

I see you looking at your watch, but I can see the clock up on the wall there and it isn't so very late. On account of my leaving tomorrow this is the only opportunity you'll be having to listen to some of the stories I can tell you, and I'm not thinking of starting off on the road at any particular time. The fact is it isn't every night I have somebody to sit around with when I get through playing. Of course some jobs there'll be plenty people waiting to come up to me and get my autograph and ask me about the tunes I played, and many's the night I have had so many people after me I couldn't hardly make it to the door, I'm telling you. But with business being so bad at this particular time it looks like things have come to be a little quieter. I see you're drinking a little. The boy that's cleaning up behind the bar can get us some more when this is all gone.

As I was saying, I had gone out to Los Angeles

before, just after I had came away from New Orleans, but that was before the days of Hollywood and the town was still just a little bitty place and I didn't think much of it at all. That must have been about 1909 or 1910. I had a fellow that I kept with me sometimes when I was doing a little hustling playing pool. I never was no kind of tough guy, and when you're doing any kind of hustling it can be a help to you to have a partner who looks like he could help you out in a fight. Now this fellow — his name was Harry, Harry Walker, and he was originally from some place over in Alabama — he couldn't do all that much if we got in any trouble, but he would put his hat down over his eyes like this, one of those old derby hats, you understand, and look at you kind of mean like, and while the boys there would be trying to figure out was this guy tough, we'd have time to get out the door.

Anyway, Harry had been to Mexico and he kept after me to go down to Mexico with him and he said there was lots of the boys had gone down there and some of them had set up businesses and they had all kind of little rackets going for them since nobody bothered whether they was colored or white. I had been playing all the clubs and the cabarets they had around Los Angeles but things was kind of slow so I thought I might go down and see what it was all about. They didn't have so many cars in those days, but Harry got us a car somewhere and we set off to drive to Mexico. Now it was hot on that road, let me tell you, and it wasn't like Louisiana. You couldn't see a tree anywhere you looked and the ground looked like it had all been burned up. Of course it was the desert, just like you see out the window of the train when you go out to Arizona, but at the edge of the desert out there in California they had the ocean.

Now that's something you don't see every day of your life and Harry said let's go down to the ocean and I know you're going to think what I'm telling you is crazy, but we pulled the car off the road and there wasn't nobody around but us, so we took off our shirts and our shoes and socks and rolled up our pants and we walked right out into the water, and Harry wasn't watching what he was doing and a wave come and landed on top of him and he got his clothes all soaking wet with that salt water. I don't know to this day why we did it, but you know how sometimes you just have enough of doing the same thing all the time and you say to yourself, I'm going to do something wild and kind of crazy. I look back at those times and all the different places I played and so forth and so on, and the fact of the matter is I don't think I let myself be crazy enough. When you're an artist you take yourself seriously. Very seriously. But right at that moment we had a yen to go in that water and we didn't let anything stop us. Of course I got a little wet too, but not as bad as Harry.

Maybe that was what started everything off in Mexico for me because I was kind of crazy all the time I was down there and that was one of the times in my life I made a mistake in my feelings. I shouldn't perhaps be telling you all these kinds of things but I know you have made a mistake in your feelings too. Everybody does if they live in this world and they get to the age where their feelings come out. But it wasn't in the beginning that everything happened. Harry and

I got down to the border and they let us through even though Harry was still all dripping wet with that salt water. We found us a little hotel right away and we got Harry dried off and then he said we should go take a look at the clubs and the eating places and so forth and so on. The name of the town we had come to was Tijuana. No doubt you've heard of it and I named one of my favorite numbers after it. At that time there wasn't much to it, just some dirt streets around the big church and then a couple of long streets with some stores and when you got around a hill there was the tenderloin district. Now the district was bigger than the town, I do believe. They had all kind of tourists which had came down from Los Angeles and San Diego and they were looking for a good time and Tijuana had whatever they were looking for. Whatever you can name in the line of pleasure you could find it there. So I said to Harry, let's find us a place where we can go in and drink a beer since all that sun has made me thirsty and Harry just waved up and down the street. We can just go into any old place we want, Harry said, it don't make no difference about colored or white in Tijuana.

Now when Harry said that I didn't know if he was serious but the next place we got to, Harry just pushes open the door and goes on inside. I didn't know what to do so I followed him and he was already up at the bar ordering us a glass of beer. Now I could see there was white men there, and white women were sitting in there too, and I expected somebody to get up and run the two of us out of there, but nobody looked at us. Then I got to the bar with Harry and the fellow standing beside him was kind of dark and the fellow behind the bar was the same color, so I said to Harry in a low voice, they got a lot of boys in here trying to pass, but they're a little too dark complexioned to get away with it, and he started laughing and said, boy you got some learning to do. They got people of all kinds in here, but those dark boys you see, they Indians, or they got some Indian blood in them. You get some fellow from the States who sees you in one of these places and he starts in on you, just you say to him that you an Indian, and if the Mexicans start in on you you just say you nothing but a Yankee and you won't get in trouble with nobody.

Now, we weren't paying much for the hotel room and we saved our money because at first I didn't like the food they had there, but we had to have some money to get along. I said to Harry, let's go find a pool room and I'll do a little hustling but Harry said no, I would just get myself all cut up and we wouldn't get anything out of it. The boys in Mexico wouldn't stand for being hustled. The fact of the matter is you have a hard time hustling if you stand out too much and since I couldn't speak Spanish and I had on the wrong kind of clothes I had as much chance of passing for a Mexican as a chicken does of being taken for a frog. But Harry knew a little Spanish and he told me to follow him and we went to one of the big houses, where they had all kinds of girls.

Most of those places were pretty low class, and they didn't have a parlor for the girls to sit in. Everybody who come in the place was expected to dance and they had a big dance floor there in the middle of the room. A lot of the fellows just came into the places to dance and get a little drunk and they had music going all the time to keep everybody happy. Now I could see why Harry told me to come with him, but the place had a couple of fellows playing guitars. I learned one thing about Mexican fellows in places like that. You give one of them a guitar and they'll kill you with it. I never heard anything in my life like the way they could play the guitar. It wasn't just chording, it was whole melodies and all type of beautiful harmonies. But Harry said to me, those fellows you think are so fine, they're a dime a dozen around here. If we can find you a place that has a piano then our troubles will be over. So we looked around and found us a place with a piano and it wasn't in too good a shape, but I could get a melody out of it and I got us some money right away because I could play the latest numbers from Los Angeles and the tourists thought very highly of my abilities as a piano player.

So we stayed on, Harry and I, with him working as my manager as he called it. And I got to like everything about it. I didn't have to think about who I was. Nobody was waiting for me to do something foolish so they could get me in trouble. Everybody was some different color so it didn't make a goddamn bit of difference that I was colored too. Of course it was just a small place, but all kinds of people came to Tijuana so I didn't feel that my talents had been hidden away. Fact of the matter is three or four weeks after we had came there Harry succeeded in getting me a job in the best restaurant in the town and I was a great success there with my own numbers. Also the public seemed to like what I gave them in the line of songs so my singing voice was as popular as my piano playing.

Now nice people came to this restaurant, not just

the whores and the gamblers and the pimps that frequented the restaurants we had been used to in the district. Nice families would come in with their daughters and their sons. High class families with all kind of good clothes and I could see that it didn't make no difference to them that I was a colored person. Some of those high class families that came into the place were darker than I was and everybody treated them with all the respect in the world, even the white people who ran the restaurant. They were white but they were Mexican and I don't like to say something like this because I'm proud of my country, but I had a better chance to make something out of myself down there than I did in my own home town of New Orleans. So of course you'd expect me to make a mistake.

The girl that started coming in to the restaurant was a very light color. If it had been New Orleans she could have passed without any difficulty whatsoever, but down here it didn't make any difference so I don't think she ever thought about being any different than I was. As far as I was concerned she was white and that's the way I treated her. She would come in and sit at a table close to the piano and I could see that she had someone who came in with her who I later found out was her mother, but this lady would sit close to the door and let this girl talk to me. She had learned a few things to say in English and I had learned how to talk in Spanish by this time so we could talk a little. Her name was Rosita or Rosalia or something like that, but I give her the name Rose and that's what I called her. Now when you have traveled around to so many places as I had you think you have seen everything, but the one thing I had never seen before was the look Rose had in her eyes. Her eyes were brown, a very light brown, and they were as soft as the feathers on a bird's stomach. She always wore very high collars and everything like that. She was very high class, but I could see in her eyes that she had warm feelings. She had dark hair, like all those Mexican women had, and she wore it pulled back onto the back of her head in what they call a bun only I don't know what name she had for it.

Now, when she had come into the restaurant for three or four days and she always sat right up close to where I was playing, she asked me if I could walk with her when I got through playing. That surprised me because I didn't expect anything like that to happen when we couldn't say more than six words to each other and that was adding up together what the two of us could say. Now they had a break in the restaurant when I didn't have to play and I suppose she knew all about that and when I got out the door she was waiting for me. So that's how it all started. We couldn't talk to each other in any kind of a way so we'd walk along the street and we'd look in the window of a store at something and she'd start laughing like it was funny and I'd get laughing right with her. She looked like she was very small, but she come up above my shoulder and when I was right up beside her she seemed to be very tall. Now I know you won't believe this when I tell you, but the fact of the matter is walking around is all we did. She'd take me up one street and then she'd take me down another street and we'd be back at the restaurant and she would stand there looking at me and then she'd go off.

Now I was making good money from all the

tourists and the rich people in the town who wanted to hear my numbers and wanted me to play especially for them and so forth and so on, and I had bought myself several suits of clothes and the very best in shoes and I had bought for myself a diamond stick pin to go in my neck tie. Even my partner Harry had got himself two or three new suits of clothes, he was making his money due to a card game he had opened up in our hotel where he played most of the night and on into the daylight. Now I don't know if it was my new clothes or if it was something about my face but I could see that there was something Rose liked and when you just come into a town and you don't know so many people and a woman looks at you then you get interested pretty quick. Now if Rose had been working in one of the houses, or if she had come into some saloon where I was working I would have told myself I got to get next to this broad, but Rose wasn't that kind of lady.

Of course, Tijuana had all kinds of music. It wasn't only guitar players. They had orchestras that played those pretty little waltzes the people are so crazy for down there and some nights they had a brass band that played in a little park close to the church, so she took me there when they had music and we would sit on a bench and nobody would take any notice of us except some people recognized me for playing the piano in the restaurant. Now Rose and I had gotten so we could talk a little and she would ask me about where I had came from and what kind of a family I had and I could see she was wanting to ask me if I was married somewhere, so one night when we were sitting on the bench and she was asking me about the places I had been and what I had left behind me, I told her I hadn't left much of anything behind me. I had never been married and I didn't have a woman waiting for me anywhere that I knew about. And she got all upset and she didn't know what to say.

Now all the time, of course, her mother always stayed somewhere around so I knew she was there. Harry had told me that the girls there, that is girls like Rose, always had somebody to go out with them as a chaperone and that's what Rose's mother was doing. But Rose was kind of disturbed on the bench there and she wouldn't look at me and I didn't want to do anything that would draw her mother's attention, so I said in a very low voice, would you come to my hotel after I get through. Now as soon as I said it I got the feeling that I should have kept it to myself. She got up off that bench and went over to her mother and the two of them went off and she never looked back in my direction and I sat there listening to that brass band up on the little platform they had playing one of those Mexican waltzes everybody loved so much.

The truth is I didn't think I would ever see Rose again and I didn't know where she lived and I didn't know how to ask anybody so I tried to get her out of my mind. But if you've ever done any traveling you know how slow the hours can go past when you don't have anything to do and you're in a hotel in a new town. And when the hours go slow you have so much time to think and every time I'd start to look out the window I'd see Rose's face. So I told myself to think about something else and then after three or four nights I came outside after my break and there was Rose. She didn't say anything but she started walking and she was waiting for me to come after her and we started walking and we didn't say anything the whole time but then when she was standing there at the door to the restaurant I felt like I must say something or she would think I was some kind of dummy. Now, you know I am a pretty fair talker but standing on that street with Rose and this time she was looking at me again with those eyes of hers I couldn't think of anything to say except to ask her if she was going to come by tomorrow night and if she did I would play her favorite numbers for her. She listened while I was saying it and then she said she would come and without having any kind of idea in my mind about what I was doing I reached up and took that diamond stick pin out of my neck tie. Now she was in one of those dresses she wore with the high collar and this dress was all in white and she had a lace shawl around her shoulders the way those women did down there and I took my diamond stick pin which I had taken out of my own neck tie and I put it on the shawl she was wearing. She kept looking at me all the time I was doing it and she didn't say anything but I could see there was a tear coming down from her eye and then she put her hand on the pin and she turned around and she went away.

Now, I can see you thinking I must be some kind of sucker, but if you could have seen that woman's eyes you would have done the same as I did. Of course, I could tell you about women I have had in this town or that town and the things they have given to me as presents and so forth and so on, but if you're out traveling around then it's some woman like Rose that will make you fall. Now my life had made me a drifter. I was always bound for someplace. People say you bound for someplace if you on the way there and I was always on the way. I was looking for that place that was big enough for me and for the rest of that night I thought I'd found it right there in Tijuana with this girl who had those lovely eyes. So when she came in to the restaurant the next night she came close down to the piano again and she just sat there smiling while I played all the pieces I had come to know which were her favorites and when I was getting up to go outside she got up with me as if she didn't care if people saw us together.

When we started walking I could see she still was wearing the tie pin with the diamond in it and when we'd gone a little way down the street she said to me, will you take me to Los Angeles? I should have thought there was something wrong about it because she couldn't say all of that in English unless somebody had helped her with it. Just to make sure I had gotten her meaning she said it to me again, would I take her to Los Angeles. So I said, alright, I would take her, if she wanted to go with me. And the fact of the matter is I wanted to go back with her and see what might happen when she was up there in my country.

Of course, Rose couldn't go anyplace without her mother and I never got a chance to say anything more to her because her mother came to the hotel where Harry and I was staying and she found Harry and they had a long talk because Harry could talk much more in their language than I could. I sat there listening and finally Harry said you better get something to put your suits of clothes in because we all are going to take a little drive up to Los Angeles. Now I wasn't thinking about anything but Rose so I went out and bought myself a suitcase, the kind of big leather ones the Mexicans make, and I told them at the restaurant I was going to go and they were very sorry to see me leave, but they told me I could come again and we started the drive to Los Angeles the next morning. I should have gotten the idea when the car pulled up to the border because Harry and I had to answer so many questions and Rose and her mother just sat in the back seat and pretended like they weren't paying any attention to what we were saying. We told the fellows there we had just came down for a day, all four of us, and when they stuck their heads in the windows and said something to Rose she talked a little English and it didn't sound so bad so after the fellows talked for a little they let us go through.

Now, Rose and her mother seemed to be arguing about something when we got back on the road again but they were looking out the window of the car at the same time and pointing to things and talking some more. Harry kept looking at me a little funny, but he didn't know all what they were saying and when he got as far as the beach he said we should stop the car and go out into the water and at first they didn't want to do it. So we got Rose out of the car and her mother came a little way after us and Rose and Harry and I started down across the beach. Now it was kind of damp on the sand and there was all kinds of stuff thrown up out of the water like the ocean was tired of everybody and it was throwing things out at them and Rose put out her hand so I could help her get over all those rough spots, and what with the way I was feeling her hand was just like her eyes. You could have led me off and wrapped me up in an old sheet and I never would have known the difference. Then Harry wanted to take his shoes off again and Rose went back to her mother while Harry and I put our feet in the waves again only Harry was careful this time and he didn't let a wave catch up to him. The fact of the matter is Harry and I weren't no better than a ten year old boy when he's trying to let a girl know he's in the vicinity. We jumped up and down in the water and we run off after the seagulls and all the time I was half looking back at Rose to notice if she was seeing all this.

It was kind of late when we got into Los Angeles, but Harry knew about a hotel, and he was able to get rooms for all four of us. I took a room by myself but Rose and her mother were together and we carried their suitcases up and we told them goodnight and Rose told me she would see me in the morning. Now I know you can see what was coming. I think I could see it too, but the fact of the matter is I had gone so soft on Rose I would have done it all for her just to have her put her hand in mine when we were walking on the beach. And of course, when Harry and I came down the next morning we didn't see the two of them and when we asked at the desk they told us they had already checked out and gone in a taxicab. When I heard that I felt very bad. I knew that Rose had just wanted to get over the border and she thought by this means she could get me to help her in her scheme. Of course when I got to thinking about it I got all hot and excited and I told Harry we should try to find them but he said they were no doubt down in the section of town where there were other Mexican people and we would have no way of knowing how to come in contact with them, and we would have a very hard time getting anybody to help us.

Now, you're wondering by this why I ever had a yen to go back to Mexico. You're probably wondering why I even told you all this story when it's just similar to the kind of story so many men could tell. Well, I want you to know the things that have come into my life and because of this I have learned my lesson. That's what we all tell each other stories for and when you hear me play one of the numbers I have wrote down in old Mexico you know what it's for. One thing that discouraged me that day I found Rose was gone was the fact that she couldn't tell me anything because she didn't know enough words. Even if I did find her I still wouldn't know what was going on. But while I was standing there one of the boys that was working at the hotel and took care of suitcases, he come up and said he had to talk to me and could we go somewhere. I could see he was Mexican and he couldn't talk so much English so I went with him off in a corner and he told me Rose had said he should say something to me about how sorry she was. Her mother had made her do it and she felt very sorry if I had misunderstood her.

The boy could talk in both languages and Rose had told him everything in Spanish. Her mother had somebody for her to marry and they were going to go to another hotel and try to find him. When he started talking I had an idea what he had to say but I still didn't want to hear it and I walked off without giving him any money, and I went back up to Harry for the rest of the day. When I did go out I saw the boy again and I gave him a dollar and said I was sorry I had been angry with him and asked him if he knew what hotel they had gone to and he said he didn't know. So I went out with Harry and we went around to the clubs and the bars and so forth and so on, and when we had came back to the hotel it was so late we didn't want to change rooms so I said goodnight to him and I went up to my room, but I could tell when I opened the door that somebody was in the room only there wasn't any light. Just the curtains all pulled back so the light from the street came in and you could see a little. It was Rose sitting there in a chair in her white dress with the shawl around her and there was a little shine from my stick pin. She wouldn't look up at me but she was trying to say things and I could see she had been sitting there trying to think of the words so she could explain to me. There was a man with property in Los Angeles and she knew him from a long time ago and her mother had arranged for everything and the man was going to come to get them tomorrow. Of course it had already came into my mind what she was going to say but what made it different was that she wouldn't do it unless she could tell me herself. I still remember Rose because of that. Then after she got through telling me she stood up and I thought she was going to go away but she had her face turned and she said she would do what her mother said but she would be thinking of me and she started to take her clothes off and while I was standing there too surprised to do anything she got into the bed. And she let me do whatever I wanted because in a manner of speaking she wanted to make it up to me for what she had done. But at the same time I could see she wanted to be there anyway.

Now, the next morning we woke up with the bed all messed up and she wouldn't look at me and I had to go out into the hall while she got her clothes on, but she let me follow along with her when she started

68

walking to the hotel where she was with her mother. And as we went along the street I could feel this bad thing happening. This was Los Angeles. I wasn't down in Mexico and I could see people staring at me because I was walking along with a white woman. One or two fellows that were passing in their cars slowed down and shouted things out to me. Rose didn't understand what they were saying, but as we got closer to the hotel where she was staying I could see her getting all nervous. Well there wasn't anything we could do about it.

We passed a store window, just like we used to do in Tijuana and she pointed to something in the window. I think it was some kind of doll, and it had a funny costume on. In the old days we would have laughed, but this time we just stood there looking down at it, both of us feeling like we should have stayed in that bed but just the same knowing that sometime we'd have to get up out of it. Then while I was standing there I heard her feet starting to take little steps and when I finally looked up she was on her way down the street with her head down and I didn't try to follow her. I just went back to the hotel and I got Harry out of bed and told him we were going back to Mexico.

When I got back to Tijuana with Harry it was no difficulty for me to take over my job at the restaurant because there was no way they could get somebody to take my place. But of course after I had been to Los Angeles, even if it was just for two or three days, I could see that Tijuana was just a little bitty place and I waited a week so as people wouldn't think I was out to fool with them and then I told Harry I had to get back because there was nothing for me in Tijuana. Harry said, you mean Rose isn't in Tijuana, and we had an argument. To get it over with I said, you're right but I have to get on the road anyway. Well, Harry said, I don't know if I want to spend the rest of my life closed up in a room with all that smoky air and those bad actors just playing cards.

So we came back to Los Angeles and that boy, I'm telling you, he couldn't get close to that ocean without wanting to get his feet in it and this time we had plenty money, so we stayed over in a little hotel that accepted coloreds and we had us a fish dinner and there was a little girl I could see was looking me over but there was two of us ready to chase after her so she went off somewhere and we didn't see her until morning. Then she came right up to our table and gave us a little smile and spun around so we could see the hobble skirt she was wearing and she said with a big smile, sleep alright you boys?

It was no trouble for me to pick up a job playing in Los Angeles since I had met so many people working in the restaurant in Tijuana and some of them were people with their own businesses up in California. But all of that which had happened with Rose had made me disappointed. Very disappointed. And I said to myself, Jelly, you think you're some kind of a big shot because you're supposed to know something about playing the piano, but there is some things you don't know anything about at all. At that time I was about twenty-three or twenty-four years old. I wasn't a kid, but I wasn't as grown up as I thought I was. I determined to leave Los Angeles and travel around the country and see if I could learn a few things.

Now one thing which was very popular then was the shows. There was shows everywhere you looked. It seemed to be the new thing for Negroes who could sing and dance to go traveling in shows. When I was growing up in New Orleans they didn't have anything like this. If Negroes did come around on a stage they always were doing a minstrel show, with everybody sitting there in a line taking their turn with songs or mugging or some kind of eccentric dancing. But what had commenced to be popular were real shows, with a chorus and costumes and sometimes there would be some kind of story to keep it going along.

Most of the shows were kind of simple. Some fellow or lady who had became known for singing or dancing would set up as the star of the show and they would have the best spots in the program and they would have some special numbers of their own that everybody was waiting to hear. The rest of the show was whatever acts they could find which would take care of comedy or dancing or whatever they needed. The big thing was always the chorus, which was the part that was new because this was a chance for those

71

people in those little bitty places where the shows played to see colored girls up on the stage. For the girls in the choruses they always looked for girls with very light skin, because that was what everybody considered to be the most beautiful. The fact of the matter is some of those girls were so light skinned you could only tell their color by looking at their hair and their eyes. Once the star of the show and his managers had everything put together they would give it a name like "Rastus Johnson" or "Delectations From Darktown" and they'd write a little bit of dialog with something in it about whatever name they had came up with and the show was ready to go.

I did so much traveling with those shows. Right at the beginning I didn't think I'd go such a long way off because I still was thinking about what I had experienced in Mexico and what I was trying to do was learn a little more so it wouldn't happen to me again. But once you have commenced to travel on the road you don't stop, which suited me at that time. I'd go out with one show and we'd get as far as Omaha or St. Louis and then I'd get in on a new show and come back to Cleveland and Columbus, Ohio, and every little place in between. I had put together an act with my being a tramp piano player who did jokes and sang songs and some tricky numbers on the piano and since I could go over singing or playing or doing comedy I could stay on the road every night of the year.

Of course I had burnt cork on my face, and my lips were all painted like they were big and white, but since everybody was doing it I didn't let it get to me. Even the famous artists like Bert Williams and Ernest Hogan and Bob Cole blacked up their faces and we all

72

could do that stage talk people liked to hear, with all the mispronunciations and the stories about preachers and watermelon and razors and shooting craps and stealing chickens. Once we got on that stage we were "coons." I suppose it all had came to be some sort of make-believe game for us. I think most of the simple colored people in the audience wanted so hard to make white people like them that they were willing to act however which way the white people wanted them to act. If the white people wanted Negroes to be "coons," alright, we would go out on the stage and act like coons and the Negroes would laugh at us for what we were doing. Of course most of the theaters we played in had seats downstairs for white people and the second and third balcony were for Negroes. So we always had white people looking at us at the same time, and the fact of the matter is the people who owned the theaters every one of them was white and they always had somebody to watch our acts to make sure we didn't do anything to upset the white people which were in the seats downstairs, since those were the tickets that cost the most and that was where they made their money.

I think the only time anybody let anything slip was when Williams and Walker — that was Bert Williams and his partner George Walker before Walker died from syphilis — got fed up with all the white fellows on the stage doing the kind of thing as they were doing but with their faces blacked up and they put out posters saying they were "The Two Real Coons." Of course, we could understand their meaning behind it but the white people who were managing the theaters didn't get it at all. Just so long as we came out on the stage with burnt cork on our faces and we pretended to be "coons," everything was alright with them. Now they didn't make the ladies black up. You know what I'm talking about. They would look at a colored face on the stage as long as it was a woman's. It was the face of a colored *man* they wouldn't accept.

Those were some times, I'm telling you. It was very often we didn't get the money we had been promised and sometimes the show would go broke and we'd be stranded, as they called it, in some town where the only hustling you could do was to break into your suitcases and sell your clothes to get back where you started. But I didn't think it was hard because I was always moving on to new places and it was at this time that I learned all the things you have to learn about women so you won't be mistaken in your feelings as I had been in Tijuana. Sometimes on the road like that we'd go out on a show with one chorus line, and we'd come back in with half the girls brand new. We always had new girls, which made people who weren't in show business very envious of us. How do you get all those girls, they would ask me, and I would give them a story about a special carpet which I had taken with me and I would unroll in front of the door to my room in the hotel where we all were staying. When I would come back from the

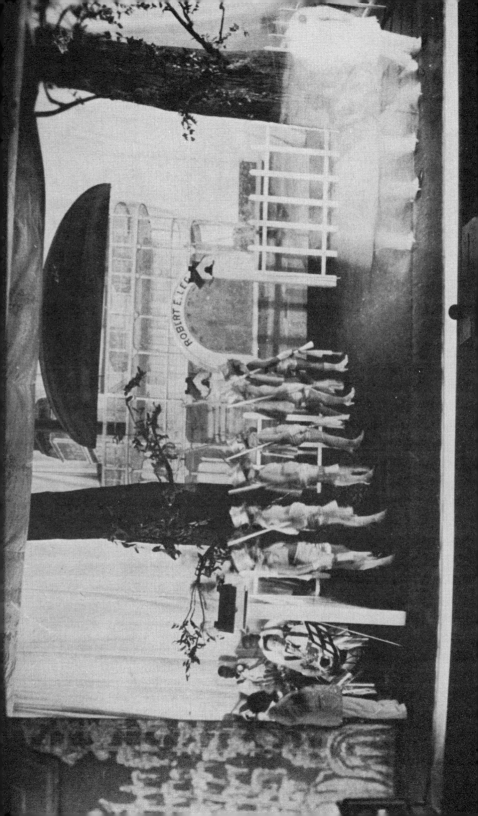

theater there would be the girls, standing there on that little carpet waiting for me. Now when I told somebody this they would get very hot because they would think I wasn't being serious with them. The truth was we were out playing our shows in those little bitty towns where nothing was going on except that every now and again a horse would run away and everybody would kind of stand around hoping it wouldn't get caught because of all the excitement it was causing.

Now if a girl was unhappy in one of those towns there wasn't much she could do about it. The only kind of work for her was to go be a maid or work in somebody's kitchen or get married, and if they couldn't find somebody to marry them they'd have to go on living at home, even if they didn't get along with everybody, and in those kind of large families everybody was sleeping together in the same bed because they didn't have any money. Sometimes when a fellow would get real salty with me and say I better tell him the truth about all those women I'd tell him something like this and he'd scratch his head and say, you always come back with nothing but pretty women and you can't tell me a pretty woman can't get the man she wants. The fact of the matter is there's just as many unhappy pretty women as there is unhappy ugly women. Sometimes it all comes from how somebody treated them when they were just girls and when they're little like that nobody knows which ones are going to be the pretty ones. The only difference between them is that a pretty woman has an easier time doing something about it.

Of course, just as soon as we'd come into a new town and we'd get off the train we'd see the girls hanging around, trying to get a look at us. Sometimes there would be so many you'd have thought someone had let a dollar bill drop on the sidewalk. And there would be all kinds, pretty ones and plain ones and thin ones and fat ones. Some of them were so homely you'd think they would be ashamed to come around and try to talk to us and some were so pretty you wouldn't believe that anybody would allow them to walk around loose on the street. Of course, we'd give the pretty ones the eye just to let them know we weren't some kind of a tomboy or anything along that line which you found sometimes among the theater people. If some of the girls had gotten themselves into some kind of trouble and it was one of those little side road places where you couldn't do anything without everybody knowing about it, then they would be looking to find some possibility for us to help them out. You didn't have to be able to do much in those kind of shows. If they could dance a little and sing a song all the way through, then we'd put them in the chorus. Of course they had to let people look at them when they were out there on the stage with nothing on their legs but their tights and for some of the girls which had it in their minds to come with us that was very hard.

And we had our side of the bargain. If we were going to take them along and let them learn some things and give them a job in the show then they had to do something for us. That's why you never could hold on to them. It was like some kind of deal you were making between you except for the fact that nothing ever was said about it. You would just look her in the eye and give her a little smile and tell her you were sweet on her and she was just the one girl you had been looking for all your life and she could see that you were saying the same thing to two or three other girls in the show at the same time, but a woman doesn't have so much choice in those things and they would let it continue until they could find something a little better or you'd come to a big city and they'd go out to look for some kind of job. But you'd have your fun and both of you would know there was something else coming along around the next corner.

Now, when I had been out on the road for three or four years people commenced saying to me that the place for me to be seen was New York City. They would listen to me play the piano and tell me, if you haven't been to New York why you haven't been anywhere at all and if you haven't played in the New York clubs and dance halls and cabarets and so forth and so on, why you're no better than a man standing out in a rainstorm who gets all soaking wet because he can't make up his mind which way he wants to run to. Now I didn't think New York was all that great because I had been so many places and I had seen so much in the way of the best things in life. I think it was somewhere around 1911 or 1912 that I first came into New York and of course I went to Harlem and in those days Harlem wasn't as far uptown as it is today. People still were living around what they called

San Juan Hill and that's where most of the cabarets were located. I had heard of some of the local piano players and some of the boys could play pretty good. Of course they didn't have the swing to it, like we did down in New Orleans, but they could finger pretty good and they had some good numbers. Eubie Blake, he was one of the best, and Lucky Roberts, he also was good. The ones you hear about nowadays, James P. Johnson and the rest, they was just kids then and they snuck in places where I played so they could learn something.

You might wonder why I'm telling you about New York when I have been telling you about my experiences with those women on the road and everything which happened to me in Mexico with Rose. Why I'm telling this is because of the stories you no doubt heard about me and all my women in New York City. The fact of the matter is I did have several women with me when I came to New York. Everyone of them was beautiful and everyone of them was young and they had the same kind of spirit as you get in a young squirrel. Frisky, is what we used to say about girls like that. Now nothing helps you stop thinking about one woman faster than another woman and I had seven or eight of them with me, dressed in the finest of clothes and two or three of them had diamonds on their fingers and when they came into a club everybody in the place would turn around to see who they were. So these fellows saw me sitting there at a table with all these women and they got a little jealous and the story they started to tell was that I was selling these women. You still hear people whispering about it today, Jelly was nothing but a pimp, he had a whole string of women. Why, I believe at that time the women in New York were so low class you couldn't have sold a thing to the boys there because they was all getting it for nothing. The musicians were going around saying that because when it came to piano playing they had to acknowledge me as superior and if they wished to step up to the pool table with me I could do the same thing to them there that I did at the keyboard. It didn't matter to me what they wanted to do, when it came to the piano and the pool table I was the person who called the tune, and once I got going why I'd walk over them like they weren't anything but bumps on the sidewalk.

Now I don't mean to say that some of these women weren't doing a little transacting. That's only natural when you got a woman in a saloon and everybody is trying to get her to be nice to them. After a while she's going to say, well, if I'm nice to you what are you going to do for me? And they come to some kind of agreement. I didn't need all of those beautiful women just sitting around with me all the night. So long as I had three or four sitting around so as to jump up and see to it the waiter brought us what we asked for I was content, and if some of the girls wanted to have a chance to meet some of the local fellows, well I didn't feel it was right to argue with them. But I never took nothing of what they made. That was strictly their own personal business. What they were was girls from the shows and if you saw me out in a night club or cabaret and you saw me sitting with a crowd of beautiful women then you would know I had just came to town with a show. Of course, there was usually one of them that was sweet on me. The fact of the matter is there might be two or three of them that was sweet on me at the same time, but I was always careful with my feelings because with those women it was here today and somewhere else tomorrow and you couldn't hold on to them any more than you could pick up water between your fingers.

Anyway, I didn't need anything like that to make money because when I came to New York I was red hot. You can ask James P. Johnson or any of them boys. I could do things on the piano they had never even thought of yet. I already said some of them could finger pretty good. They knew their music. Where I had the advantage on them which they could not overcome was that I was doing my own music. It wasn't just special tunes or little melodies which you no doubt have heard people take claim for when they know I was the one that brought them here. I had created a whole new style of music that was strictly my own. It wasn't ragtime. You could take ragtime and put it inside my style and you'd have room left over beside it. My style had ragtime in it, but it also had other things. I didn't just play the blues, because my style had room for the blues and when you put the blues into it you still had room beside that. I had put everything into my music, then added some of my own ingredients. So when I came to town with my music I caused those boys to quit which was considered the best they had in town. The reason they couldn't do what I did was they thought they could get their style from books and from music which was wrote down on paper. You find people all the time, they feel a little uneasy with themselves. They can't say, I'm this or that, they pretend to be something else.

Now all over the United States they had Negroes that didn't want to say they were Negroes. I knew who I was because I had been down there with those low-class kind of people. Even though my family came from the highest class of Creole society if somebody said to me, boy there's some kind of music going on and you should get those ears of yours to where you can listen, I always had it in my mind to go to that place even if it was down in some honky tonk where all the roughest people hung out. So I heard all that those type of musicians were playing and I heard what they were singing and I even took it upon myself to learn all those eccentric dances you see on the stage today. Hell, if it wasn't for the customers still hanging around I could show you things that would knock your eyeballs out. And I wasn't ashamed of all that. I wasn't afraid somebody was going to come up to me and say, Jelly, can't you do nothing better than that low down stuff? I wasn't afraid to play hot music. I wasn't afraid that people would look down on me if I played piano with plenty swing and plenty rhythm. I wasn't afraid to mix in melodies I had heard in those low class places. If some of those numbers had been any lower down I would have had to get down on the floor on my hands and knees and put my ear right on the floorboards to hear them.

So when I came into the famous night spot in New York City, which was Wilkins' cabaret where all the best people in town gathered, I was nothing less than what you might call a sensation playing in my style. At that time they always had an orchestra at Wilkins. It was one of those orchestras with the mandolins and violins that Jim Europe was sending out around New

York. And I and my women, I say my women although they had just came into town with me in a show where they danced some numbers in the chorus, we sat down and I called the manager of the place over to the table and I said to him that he could let the orchestra take a break because I proposed to take over at the piano. The fellow said, you crazy? Can't you see we got a whole orchestra up there and you want to take over by yourself on the piano?

I had taken the liberty of explaining the situation to the ladies I had brought with me and I gave them a signal behind my back and they started crying out that they wanted to hear me play. One of them, which was a tall, real good looking girl with wavy hair, came up to the manager with her face all pouty and she looked him right in the eye and said, you mean you're not going to let us have a good time in your cabaret? So we had a little argument, and finally the manager told the band to go take a smoke and he made a little speech to the public about how they were going to hear a guest artist and then he said to me in a low voice, go make a fool out of yourself, nigger. Now he was darker colored than I am, but what he was saying was that I was acting low class.

Well that made me even hotter to get to the piano stool to show them what I could do. Of course I came up to the piano just like I always did. I took off my overcoat which I had hanging around my shoulder and I folded it back very carefully so that everybody in the place had a chance to see that striped lining which was made of real silk and I laid it across the top of the piano. Then I made a little show out of dusting the piano stool even though the boy from the orchestra had been sitting on it up until I had came onto the bandstand, and I stretched my hands out, shooting the cuffs, as they called it, so people could get a look at my diamond cuff links, and all the time the girls were calling out my name and the customers which had filled up every table in the place were getting very curious to see what I could do. Even the members of Europe's orchestra hung around at the kitchen door because they wanted to see if I had something or was I just going to make a fool of myself.

Now my usual way when I was starting off in a new town was to tease them a little with one of my specialty numbers and maybe sing a song or two, but when you were in New York you couldn't take time like that. People make up their minds in a hurry in New York and I knew if I was to go over I would have to knock them down with my first number. You have no doubt heard me play my famous tune which I have gave the name to it of "Fingerbuster" because it is without a doubt the most difficult piano piece there is in the world to play. That tune sounds more modern than anything else going around today, but the fact of the matter is I had wrote that tune many years ago and I had it ready. I played a little chord just to let everybody know I knew where the keys were at and then I commenced to playing "Fingerbuster" at a very fast tempo. I won't say I was the only one who did this trick, but we didn't sit straight at the keyboard. Instead, if we were in a battle of music as it's called, we'd sit with our bodies turned away and one knee over the other and we wouldn't even look at the keys while we were playing. I tell you when I got through the place went crazy.

The fellows with Europe's orchestra had never gotten no further than the kitchen door and they never had lit up their cigarets. One of them was standing there with the cigaret in his mouth and he had struck the match to light it and when I started playing he forget entirely what it was he was doing and he let the match burn down until it singed his fingers.

Once I had their attention, as you might say, I followed it with my specialty, "The Jelly Roll Blues," with the little tango part I had picked up in New Orleans where they had so many fellows come in off the boats from the islands like Jamaica and Cuba, and the girls had heard me play it many times and some of them had a little dance that went with it and they stood up and started swaying and people started beating on the tables and I thought the manager would swell up and burst that man was so crazy. But I said to myself, fine, you can call me that name, but what I'm playing is the real Negro music and if you didn't know about it before then it's only right that somebody should come in and show you to your face how much you have missed. The tall girl went up to him, still dancing, and said, how does that suit you now, and he got so angry he went out of the room and left me there to do what I wanted. Of course, I let the orchestra come back after a while but I tell you the truth is they came back walking like whipped dogs. They kept looking down at the floor and they didn't want to see me. So just to let them know they had been fooling with a shark I put a five dollar bill in the box they had there as a kitty and thanked them for letting me come up and play for the audience. Then just when they started to play one of their own numbers, a waltz or something like that, I got up and took all the ladies downtown with me to get us something to eat.

I don't know what kind of life you've had, but I can tell you have all different manner of things to try out on account of you still are young. I suppose the reason things were so different for me was due to the fact that I had commenced traveling when I hardly was out of short pants and I had to keep a hat on my head so people wouldn't see that I still was wet behind the ears.

Now I wasn't the only one who was on the road. In those times so many things seemed to be changing and everywhere you'd go you'd find people on the move to be where the changes were happening. You'd stay in a town someplace and you'd make the acquaintance of some of the fellows there and you'd go away and you'd come back a month later and you'd ask what had happened to them and people would tell you they'd packed their suitcase and gone off someplace else. Now one reason a lot of people stay home is they're afraid to take the first step. I had taken that first step so many years ago it didn't look like I'd ever learn to stay in one place. So after a time I decided to give up the business with the shows even with all the success I had been having in every city where I had appeared. I had been to some of those places so many times, the people taking tickets at the door had taken to calling me by my first name so I knew it was time to find some new place where I could display my talents. Of course I wasn't intending to give up my piano playing. That was always my ace card when I had run out of luck at other things, as can happen to anybody from time to time, no matter how much of a big shot he thinks he is.

I considered where I would go and I determined to leave New York alone because of all that snow and so many other piano players. Now some of the boys were saying that Los Angeles was coming into some kind of a boom time. The business of making movies just had commenced and there was a lot of business which had came from the United States Navy and there was work in the oil wells and with the war in Europe coming on it looked like a place where plenty money could be made by somebody who had the talents that the people were looking for. In a manner of speaking you might say we were pioneers out there in Los Angeles. I don't mean it in the way of the fellows who went out with plows and wagons and a mule and put up the houses and so forth and so on. Our part in being pioneers was bringing out all sorts of entertainment for the people there when they had finished with their work, and they were out on the street looking for a good time. I say "we" because I took on partners in Los Angeles and I had plenty jobs playing in the little cabarets and night clubs and we had opened up our own place down on Sixth Street. My partners were two boys I had worked with in a road show. Their names were Spikes. The Spikes Brothers they were called. We had all worked together with the McCabe Minstrels playing in St. Louis around 1911. They had a little orchestra playing in the dance halls out there on Central

Avenue or in a place that wasn't much better than a joint, the Penny Dance Hall, it was called. It was down there on Ninth Street, I believe. Anyway, we got together and set ourselves up in the music business and we hired out bands and took care of helping people to get their tunes copyrighted, which was very important because there was so much stealing going on you didn't dare to play your best numbers out in public until you had got your name on the papers for fear of somebody beating you to them.

When I first started I didn't have a band of my own, because as I stated before, I was a whole band by myself. Why would anybody pay for five or six musicians when they could get me to do the job all by myself? Once I had established my name and I became known for what I could do I would walk into any club in town and the fellow there would get up off the piano stool and let me take over. Once things had commenced to be very successful there, which was when the war started, if the management of such and such a club requested me to lead an orchestra at their place then I would put a bunch together and they would play my numbers. I'm telling you, the people would stand in line to put money in the kitty, as they called the box we had on the bandstand for our tips, in order that we would play the numbers they requested which was always one of my specialties. Of course even in those days, when everything was going so good, I still wouldn't stay put. I'd take it in my head to travel to someplace like San Francisco or Portland or Seattle and before you could turn around you would find me there. Of course, if I was traveling with an entire orchestra I would have to wire ahead so as to have some job waiting when we got there, but if I was on my own I didn't need to send word since I was so well known I didn't have to do anything but show my face and the word would spread and before you could say another word I'd have all kind of jobs there for me.

Now that things had commenced to be so big out there I wasn't content just to be playing the piano. I had the music business with the Spikes Brothers and I was partners in one or two saloons which had needed some name to go under to get themselves started and I had helped some ladies which had taken it into their minds to set up in business for themselves, which also put them in the line of being pioneers since everything in the line of pleasure there was very primitive.

I had so much money in those days! I always had a roll of bills in my pocket as big as your fist and on the outside was a one thousand dollar bill. If some sport wanted to shoot a little pool with me I would let the betting get heavy and then I would take out that bill and lay it on the table and you could see the boy's face go white like his heart had stopped beating. When he had seen that, I couldn't lose. Even if he tried to shoot against me he would be seeing that thousand dollar bill and thinking about what would happen if he lost and his hand would begin to quiver like the leaves on the trees. Of course I always liked to have a little flash when I sat down at the piano and I had my diamond stick pin and my diamond cuff links, but I said to myself it was time to give the boys a real heart attack when they tried to engage me in a battle of music, so I went to the dentist and told him to put diamonds in my teeth so they'd shine when I

90

turned around to give people my smile. I even went to the tailor shop, which was the same person that was designing all my clothes and I said, I want you to take these diamonds in my hand here and put them on my garters that hold my socks up. I want to feel those diamonds on my legs. The fact of the matter is they were good times for all of us out there. I had so many suits of clothes I had to rent another room just to hang them all in the closets.

When the war came it looked like everybody got some kind of a job and they didn't care what they did with their money. They went out for a good time. And of course, if there was anything going on, if somebody needed to get in touch with somebody else, or if they wanted to meet any of the girls who were in off the road from the shows, I was in on it because I knew everything that was going on. If I had just sat at that piano I would have had very tired fingers by the time a week had gone by, I'm telling you. So I always kept my eye out for anything else that I could hustle. Some of the other boys out there could play a little so you could find anything in the line of entertainment. Sonny Clay could play pretty good piano though if he would try to play at my tempos his fingers would get mixed up like it had got too hot for them and each one of them wanted to run some different direction to get away, and Fred Washington was another one of the boys that could play a little. So I could keep things going by bringing in one of these other fellows if I wanted to take a trip.

The truth is, life was very good in Los Angeles at that time. I had a big car and when I wanted to go around town I had my old friend from the Tijuana days, Harry, to drive me and we'd go around and see if there was anything going on or maybe offer to give a lady a ride anywhere she might want to go. It always seemed to be warm enough for us to go around in our shirt sleeves, although when it come time for us to go to the job I always had the latest in style and maybe a hundred dollar suit of clothes so the boys could see I was doing alright. Now the clothes make me remember a story you no doubt have heard before but if you haven't heard it you will certainly appreciate it.

I had grown up in New Orleans with all those swell fellows in their fancy clothes and their trousers so tight they couldn't bend their knees when they stopped to talk to you. They would just hold themselves against the side of the building so that their trousers wouldn't get wrinkled. And I would say to people in Los Angeles, you think you putting on a show here, but you haven't seen a thing until you've seen New Orleans. The fact of the matter is I thought about New Orleans every now and then. I hadn't been back there for many years and I still had my godmother and my sisters living there and I thought of them the way anybody thinks about his family, even if they were kind of disgusted with me for being a piano player. I always said I would go back and let them see how well I was doing, but I had

92

the big car then and it was too hot to drive over that desert even though the car I had was one of those touring cars with the canvas top. I always could take the train, but when you got onto the train you'd meet up with your old friend Jim Crow again and he'd say to you, no, you don't want to sit down in the car here that's nice and clean and has a washroom at the end of it. I have a special car just for you. Now it's not so clean, maybe, and some of the people in it are kind of rough, but that's where you and me are going to sit. Now you could say, no Mister Crow, I don't like the looks of this place, but he'd just shake his head and take you by the arm and you'd go sit down where Jim Crow put you. So I never did get back to New Orleans.

The fact of the matter is, it was the war that was bringing all the money to the cabarets out in Los Angeles but it did just the opposite to New Orleans. I would think sometimes about all those elegant sporting houses and the crystal chandeliers and the fancy carpets on the floor and all the elegant furniture and all those girls they had in the houses there on Basin Street, but while the war was going on the government closed the whole district down. If someone had told me the district would be gone someday I would have said that man was crazy, but there it was. Of course the girls found places to go, and maybe the new places they were working didn't have all that fancy furniture, but they had what the customers needed. For some of the boys playing music, though, things got kind of slow and they started to travel around. My partners and I had one of the bands working for us out in Los Angeles and that was the orchestra of Kid Ory, which had been one of the popular orchestras in New Orleans before things closed up. And of course it looked for a while like everywhere you went there was somebody else from New Orleans. The fact of the matter was, the New Orleans musicians were very well respected for what they could do at that time and they could always get themselves some kind of job.

Just at that time there was a notoriety for the New Orleans style of jazz on account of the Dixieland Band and the records they were making stealing all our tunes like "Tiger Rag" and all those uptown blues they gave new names to, and that was what made everything from New Orleans so popular. Of course I had written some of those tunes myself and the ones which I hadn't wrote I had played and of course I knew how New Orleans music should be played in the correct way, so I said to myself I'll get an orchestra and show everybody how to do it. Now I knew that everybody in New Orleans was looking for a job and I decided I would get some of those New Orleans boys to play for me, I was working at Baron Long's Cafe and I told them I would bring them one of those hot New Orleans outfits. I asked around to everybody I could find who had just came from New Orleans to ascertain who was the best at that moment and they said the best one to get was Buddy Petit. I had never heard him play, but I knew he was from New Orleans so I sent him a telegram telling him to bring his boys and come to Los Angeles.

All the time they were on the train I was thinking I was going to have to look real sharp when they got to Los Angeles because those New Orleans boys all were very particular about the way they dressed, so when they came in the door of the Cafe I had on one of my best suits of clothes and I had on a genuine silk necktie with a diamond for a stickpin and a shirt which was made for me by the best tailor in Los Angeles. Now I took one look at that bunch of boys and I started laughing so hard I had to sit down on a chair to keep from rolling over on the floor. That was the sorriest bunch of rubes I had seen since I was out on the road with those shows I was telling you about. Buddy was in some kind of a suit, but it was made out of some kind of material that had great big green squares in it. The rest of them had on coats that didn't match their trousers and they had on those real tight trousers, but they were wearing them cut short so you could see their rolled socks, and they had on striped shirts with neckties that looked like they had been made a present of them by blind people at a fire sale. I'm telling you they would have done better to have told people they were coming to be in a circus.

Now, I have to give them something, they could play the style music people were looking for, but they looked so bad people would look at them and start to smile. When they came in the door I couldn't see any cases for their instruments and I asked them where they had left them and they said they were packed away and they had put their cornets and clarinets and so forth and so on in their suitcases. So when it was time for them to come to play I said, what you going to do then? People will think it's very strange if you come in the door with a suitcase. They said no, they would bring their instruments in a sack. And that's what they did! They come in the door and they had everything in paper sacks or wrapped up in a newspaper. Now I had been thinking about New Orleans and I had been remembering the old days

95

and when these boys came in that door I told myself I could forget about New Orleans, I had moved on and I couldn't go back to that life again.

The part that comes next is what you no doubt have heard before. The music part of it wasn't going so bad, but they didn't want to listen when I tried to tell them the right way to do everything. You had to play for many hours at a place like Long's. It was down there in Watts and that was a nice section of town and plenty of big spenders came in at all hours of the night. The custom was for the musicians to take a little break about one in the morning and have a meal so they could continue. Now they have everything in the way of delicacies down in New Orleans, but these boys acted just like they had been out on a plantation. I tell you they were so green, if they had stood out in a field long enough, corn would commence to sprout out their ears. For a night or two they sat out at the table which was set up in the kitchen for the musicians and they kind of pushed the food around on their plates and I could see them talking to each other. They didn't think what they were getting had the right seasoning. They missed their own kind of cooking.

So the next night we start doing some numbers and after a while I begin to smell something from the band stand and I look around and the boys had brought a pan of red beans and rice and they had it sitting up on a can and they had started a little fire in the can to warm up their meal. They thought they were playing for some country people out by a levee somewhere. When I saw that I jumped up from the piano stool and I started to curse them out, but the fact of the matter was it was so ridiculous seeing what they were doing that I just started laughing so hard people thought I had gone crazy. I couldn't get a word out so I just pointed and the public came up to the bandstand and they kind of crowded around bending over the little railing we had there to see what was going on, and they saw that pan of red beans sitting on top of the can and I thought they would never stop laughing. I'm telling you people had tears coming down their cheeks and they would try to say something and then they would just point at those boys who were still sitting there with their instruments and they would start laughing again.

It must have been the best part of an hour before I could get everything quiet enough so we could go on with our show, and people still kept laughing when they got to thinking about it again. When we got finished I could see the boys were kind of hot and they kept talking with their voices low so I wouldn't hear. Then Buddy Petit came up to me and he was a little fellow so I wasn't afraid of him but he said they were going to go back to New Orleans that night. And he told me that if ever I were to go to New Orleans again he would kill me himself or he would ask some of his friends to do it and some of the hardest boys in New Orleans were his friends and they would kill me for five cents or as a favor to him, it didn't make no difference to them. And they went out the door with the steam still coming up out of their shirt collars they were so hot. Of course I have never been back to New Orleans so I don't know if he was telling the truth or not, but they have some tough babies there and if I do go back again I'll send somebody on ahead to tell me what I can expect.

I know you're sitting there thinking to yourself, Jelly spends his nights telling stories about himself and the things which have happened to him on the road, but the truth is, having you sit here with me like this has caused me to go back into my memory to some of those old days. You're not doing a thing but going through your memories when you start in telling stories. The fact of the matter is when I'm remembering back like this I'm looking to see the ways I have been different from anybody else and I ask myself if I could have done anything a little different. Of course we're all going to come out at the same place at the end, but there's another way where every man is just like every other man. Everybody would like to be known and have fancy suits and make plenty money and so forth and so on, but that can't be, so they hang around waiting for somebody to tell them about it and that's almost as good. That's why I have so many people come up to me and want me to tell them about what I have done or what I have seen. They can listen to me and at the same time what they're thinking in their minds is that it's them who is doing these things I'm telling them. I don't need to play the piano or sing for people. I can do them just as much good by me talking, and that makes it easier for them to accept the things in their life which would be very discouraging.

Of course, this is something I have to tell on myself. There's many a man I meet who could tell me things about his own life which would be new to me. All those years when I was just a kid and I was on the move I never had time to think about having a family. I left out of my home in New Orleans so early I wasn't thinking along those lines and when you have led a life like mine with so many notoriety ways of doing things and you associate with so many different classes of people something like that doesn't come into your head. Now I have Mrs. Morton, my wife, who is staying in New York at this time, and I will relate her story when I have finished telling you about my Los Angeles days, but we have married in later years and due to times being so tough she can't follow with me just at this time and we never did have any children. So perhaps this will be something which you can relate to me when we meet again.

What caused me to think about these things was something else that happened to me in Los Angeles. There was a woman which I had taken it in my mind to settle down with in town. Her name was Anita Gonzales, and she was one of the most beautiful women you'd ever want to meet. You no doubt have heard my tune "Mama 'Nita." Well that was a number I named after her. She was the sister of Bill Johnson, who played the bass with me and we had worked together down in New Orleans. With a name like that some people thought she was Mexican, but she had been married before this time. I also had known her in New Orleans, where her family was all Creoles and very high class. With things going so good in Los Angeles I thought about Anita again and I heard from somebody that she was living out there, but her brother wouldn't tell me where to find her, on account of all the women I had been associated with and the gambling and so forth. But I happened to meet her mother on the street one day and she told me Anita was living in a little bitty place over in Nevada which was called Las Vegas. So I went up to see her and she was glad to see me so she came back to Los Angeles and set up a little hotel.

Her mother was an understanding woman and she let Anita and I move into an apartment with her. When things had eased up a little at her hotel then Anita would follow me to the night club or the café where I was playing so she could hear my music. I never let her dance with anybody for fear some of the fellows would get the wrong idea about her. She always sat up on the band stand with me, right beside the piano. If I had a little orchestra with me sometimes the customers would take it into their minds that she was sitting there waiting to sing a number and they would lean over the railing and tell me, you better let her sing or she'll go home on you, but I just laughed and told them she wasn't going home just at that time.

Sometimes when I was on the road to San Francisco or Portland I would take her along with me and she would wear the most beautiful kind of dresses and we always traveled with a trunk so she could have a different dress for every night, and she would sit alongside of me and people could see how beautiful she was. Of course she was like all those women from New Orleans, she was a little peppery, and sometimes she would get hot with me on account of some other woman or staying out when I was shooting a game of pool, but once she had said everything she was going to say then she would quiet down and I could come back home again.

Of course, you're younger than I am and you no doubt have not traveled around the country like I have, but probably you already have some woman somewhere that you think about sometimes. I don't suppose there's a man living who doesn't have a woman he remembers from some place or other. Even if that man is contented with his wife and loves her very much and he never looked another woman in the eye, you start to ask him and he'll tell you there was a girl who sat beside him in school or there was a woman he saw out on the street in a new dress, or once somebody he knew brought a pretty girl to a party and he got to say five words to her. He remembers her, even if it all seems like some kind of dream he had. If you asked them, women probably would tell you the same thing, except that's not the kind of a thing a woman's supposed to do, and they no doubt would be too shy to say anything about it. They remember some man from somewhere, even if it's just some fellow who sat across from them when they rode the street car to work or somebody they held hands with at a church picnic. And they never forget him. That's just as true for me as it is for anybody else. I still remember Anita Gonzales and I haven't seen her again from that time to now. Now my wife Mabel, I also keep her in my mind, even though she is up there in New York at this time. Sometimes she comes down to stay for a little while and of course I keep her in a very luxury apartment in Harlem with everything of the finest quality. But the truth is I still think a little of Anita Gonzales every now and then and all those times we had together in Los Angeles.

What it was caused me to leave Los Angeles was my business partners, the Spike Brothers. Now, we were supposed to be doing everything together and we were copyrighting some of the tunes we had been playing. Right off they had a hit with a number called "Someday Sweetheart". Part of that number was a strain I had been playing when I first had came to town. The fact of the matter is you could say I had a hand in the number all the way through on account of I was a much better musician than either of those boys who knew about as much about what they were doing as a drunk man trying to make music with a fiddle bow and a saw. Then they had taken another number of mine which I had been playing for many years and they wrote some two-bit words to it about missing the state of Michigan, which is known for an animal called the wolverine and they changed the title a little bit to call it "Wolverine Blues" and they put down on the music that it was wrote by Jelly Roll Morton and the Spikes Brothers. Now the only thing the number had going for it was my music. You hear that number played by every hot orchestra in America today and not one of them sings those words. I don't think I can sing them all the way

102

through myself.

Before I knew anything about it they had sold this number with their name on it to the Melrose brothers in Chicago, who had a music shop there and were on the lookout for something new. So I said to myself, I should go to see the Melrose brothers myself and let them in on the truth about "Wolverine Blues" as they were calling it. It was too late for me to change it back to my own composition, but if they liked that number then they no doubt would like some of my other numbers and we could do some business together. As I told you before, every place starts to feel kind of small to me after a while and things had started to slow down a little in Los Angeles, and when I get a kind of a yen to go some place I'm like a leaf that's picked up in the breeze. I just blow along with it. I didn't want to leave Anita, but she had her hotel and her mother was very content to stay in California where it was warm, so we said goodbye and we looked each other in the eye and we said we'd meet again when I had my business straightened out and I could come back to Los Angeles.

I had looked around Chicago a couple of times before the war, but in those days it was very quiet. I had came there to play the piano and maybe get a job with a show, but things were so slow I did most of my hustling in the poolrooms and I had to break my back bending over those pool tables to get out of town. But things had changed in Chicago and that was another reason for me to go there. At that time there had started to be phonograph record companies which were producing what they called "race" records, and they were putting out blues and what they called jazz and so forth and so on, and those companies were in Chicago. We had tried something along that line in Los Angeles, but I could see that it was too little bitty a place for us to do anything. Now some of those other boys were getting in on it in Chicago and I said to myself, hell, if those boys are doing something with that little bit of talent they got then I can walk in there and take over with my own tunes and my own style of playing the piano. And that's what I did.

I came into Chicago sometime about 1923, in the spring of the year. I had already known what Chicago was like in the winter, so I waited until the weather had turned warmer before I made the journey. I had all my suits of clothes and shirts and ties with me, but I didn't have that one thing you need to have in Chicago if you're going to make it through the winter, and that is a big overcoat to go over the top of everything else. I intended to have a tailor make that up for me when I got to town. Of course I went to the little store the Melrose brothers were running as soon as I got there, and to let them see they had somebody special to deal with I dressed up kind of like a cowboy. I had just came in from California so I thought I would let them see something different and when I walked into their store I was wearing a cowboy hat and a red bandana. Then before they could think of anything to say I sat down and started playing the piano and that was all they needed to hear. Now there was a lot of different kinds of music in Chicago at that time. They had every style of music you could think of except for my style and I found out that they were ready to accept it. I won't tell you about my success in Chicago. That's something that is known about everywhere in the world where there is music. I let them get my style down on phonograph records and before another day could go by I was famous.

Now, when it started with the records there was one thing which nobody thinks about anymore because they've forgotten it. In the beginning there was something mixed in it that was just as important to people as the money. For Negroes in America the records meant they had something they could be proud of. All the time the white people were telling us we couldn't have the things they had or we couldn't live like they did, and at the same time they wouldn't let us have anything of our own. As fast as we'd get something they'd take it away for theirselves. Some fellow would do a little dance on the street corner for pennies and before he knew it he'd hear about some white fellow up on the stage with that cork on his face doing his dance. We had ragtime and what happened to that? It was taken over from us. We had jazz and the Dixieland Band came along and put their name on it just because they were white. Right at the very start of the race records, I'd say that was about 1920, the white people which was in charge of everything still tried to make us play like they wanted, but then they could see that what was selling to Negroes was something that was their own. Once they'd let people hear Bessie Smith and King Oliver and the records which I had made they couldn't ever take them away again. The Negro people said these are ours and we're going to keep them.

I know you won't believe this, but it was hardly anybody at first really understood what was happening. They had little stores and music shops and so forth and so on, where you went to buy the records, but most people bought them in ordinary dime stores where they had a bin for records and the new records would come in every week and they'd have a machine there where you could play them. Out in the country they had them in the general stores or you could send in a coupon from the newspaper and get the record you wanted. Now when the colored people started seeing that the artists were Negroes they didn't hardly know how to act. Sometimes some of those boys would feel so proud about it they'd just go and stand around the counter and look at one record after another, and they'd get somebody to play them every record in the place until the people got wise that they didn't have any money to buy nothing. And of course the companies started to do a little advertising because they could see how well they were doing, and when they put pictures on the outside of the records, on that paper cover that they come in, they didn't make nobody put on black face make-up.

I know you listen to some of the records we made back in those days and they sound very poor. Some of them were so bad, I'm telling you, the fellows that made them must have wished they were working down in the bottom of a coal mine when the records came out and everybody could hear them. But at that time they were the first to be doing it, and that was all anybody cared about. I know there are people today who don't want to listen to any of those early things, they say you have to be up to the minute all the time, but when you think about what they meant to the people who were buying them, then you come to see it all in a different way. Very different. I had to learn in the beginning myself. Of course nobody could tell me anything about playing the piano and when the Melrose brothers gave me my chance I just naturally did what I was supposed to do. But the fact is when I made my first little things with a band we had a hell of a time getting it all together so it sounded like anything, and when it had came out I couldn't believe myself what it sounded like. But I learned.

That's why everything is always changing on those early records. We were learning so fast. We'd write one arrangement for a tune and we'd go to the studio and put it on the record so we could hear it and right away hear things how we could do it better and we would want to come right back again and do something different. You couldn't keep up with how fast we were learning. Of course the music was right there, in us. Negroes had been making up music for so long we had everything there inside us. We just didn't know how to get it out, and it never was any kind of music that you could write down all of it on paper. You could get some of it, and I myself was considered one of the best when it came to getting down the true sound of jazz on paper, but if you took a blues or one of those type of number there was no way you could put it down in notes. It was phonograph records that gave us our music.

Of course, everything in Chicago was changing just as fast as the music was. Most of the Negro people there hadn't been up North more than a year or two. They had came up for the jobs that started during the war. They got jobs in the steel mills or jobs in the places making uniforms or in the slaughter houses. There was plenty jobs in the beginning and you can believe those people wanted to get out of those two-bit towns down in the South where they couldn't go out behind the house without having some white man go see what they were doing. Now they were glad to get out of there and take a job where they could make some real money, but they missed things down there and that was one reason they wanted to have us come play in the cabarets and the night clubs and also that was why they bought so many records. If they got to feeling a little blue because they were all alone in Chicago they could listen to one of those tunes they remembered from down home and that would serve to make them feel a little bit better.

A lot of the jobs which people had came to find were in the steel mills way down in the south end of Chicago and the stock yards were down to the south so the South Side is where a lot of the people came to stay. Out along those streets like Michigan Avenue or Dearborn or Wabash Avenue there was the mansions which had been owned by very wealthy white people but they had moved out and the colored people moved in. Now it got to be so many people from the South down in some of those neighborhoods you'd listen to people talking out on the street and you'd think you were back in Mississippi. Everything looked different for those people and they had some money and they wanted to have a good time.

Of course when everything in your life changes so

fast it's hard to know how you supposed to act and for a lot of those people it was very hard. They had come up in some worn out cabin with holes in the roof and nothing but dirt on the floor and down there they didn't hardly see anybody except when they came into town to buy some groceries and before they know it, everything's different. And there wasn't nobody to help them out. Even if they had a job and they had a place to stay down on the South Side they didn't come any closer to white people than they did down in Mississippi, and I think for some of them they got further away. So they had to do everything for themselves and some of those people had it hard, I'm telling you.

Now, when I came into Chicago from Los Angeles I determined to find a place to live where I wouldn't have to devote any time to taking care of it, so I looked for a boarding house instead of an apartment. I thought that at first it would enable me to spend more time out looking for opportunities in the music line. And I succeeded in finding a place the first day I was there down on South Wabash. Now the people there were the kind which I have been telling you about, just up from Mississippi or some place that was even further out in the country. And the place had a landlady. When I tell you about her you'll understand all those people and what they were feeling back in those days.

Her name was Mildred, Mildred Washington, and she was from some little bitty town outside of Clarksdale. She didn't want to tell me the name of it even though I had hoboed through that part of the country on my way to Memphis in 1908. I never did know where Mildred got the money to buy the boarding house, but she talked sometimes about some man that had been very nice to her and it didn't take much to set up a place as a boarding house and if you knew anything at all about taking care of people then the place would make a little money for you and you would do alright. Now, this Mildred from Mississippi, she had taken on airs about her on account of the boarding house and on account of she had been in Chicago for almost four years, and she was of the opinion that she knew everything everybody needed to know about damn near everything in the world. Sometime when she would get to talking she would remind you of flies hanging around a dead cat. There was no way you could get rid of her.

Of course, I was from New Orleans and that made a big difference to Mildred. She knew that people in New Orleans had came up knowing about the world and they could get along with all classes of people and so forth and so on, and it didn't hurt that I was a musician. At that time there were so many boys in town playing music who had came from New Orleans. King Oliver had his band there and Louis Armstrong had came to town to be with Oliver, and Johnny Dodds was there and Kid Ory had came in from Los Angeles and there was Zue Robertson and Freddie Keppard and Albert Nicholas and Johnny Lindsay. So many of them, I can't recall all the names. I had been away from New Orleans for many years, but I still was in touch with some of the boys and I played some of the same tunes and of course they had all heard of me. Now when Mildred saw how well I was accepted by everyone and what kind of clothes I was wearing she began to give me little

looks over the table when she'd be bringing in breakfast and if I wanted a little something more to go with a meal I could always count on her to come up with it.

When I tell about her it sounds like Mildred was some illiterate woman from out in the country, which no doubt she was, but I have to say one thing for her, she was one of the most beautiful women God himself ever put down on this earth. She had a face that would make an angel cry and she had the kind of figure that nobody could take their eyes off of her. She wasn't too big, you understand. She had just enough of everything. Of course she was dark complexioned, which everybody was from that part of Mississippi, but she wasn't too dark. Somewhere back in the family somebody had came along and lightened them up and she had bright skin. When she would start talking about how much she knew about and how swell her boarding house was and how she was such a grand lady, those country fellows would just stand there with their eyes on that figure of hers and they wouldn't hear a word she said.

A lot of the boys in the boarding houses did get pretty down sometimes. I don't know if you've ever been along Wabash or Prairie or those streets down there. Those sidewalks just go straight up one side and down the other, and there are all those dark old buildings, one close in beside the next. You could walk up and down those streets for maybe ten miles and one street would look like all the others. Of course up on Michigan Avenue there were all those mansions, but along the rest of the streets there were just those apartment buildings. For those boys who had spent most of their lives out on some farm where the most they had around them was four or five more shacks looking just like theirs it could get pretty tough. The wind would start blowing and it would get cold and they'd have to stay in their rooms because it was too icy to go walking around. It was all dark and there'd be snow piled up on the streets and what they were used to was sunshine and working out in the open.

On Friday and Saturday night they'd spend a little money to give themselves a good time. They'd get on their best suit of clothes with the new watch chain they just had bought and their shiny new shoes and they'd come out to the night clubs to hear us play. I'm telling you, sometimes I used to feel sorry for them. Of course they had to order drinks, and this was in the Prohibition time so strictly speaking they shouldn't have been drinking anyway, so the gangs that was running the speakeasies, as they called them at that time, charged very high for everything. So these boys would come in wearing their best clothes and they'd put down a lot of money to get themselves a drink and sometimes they'd find a woman to talk to, and just about that time, just when the night was starting to get a little wild, I'd see them begin to get sleepy. They'd begin yawning and they'd lean back in their chairs and their heads would tip back and their new hats would fall down on the floor and that would wake them up a bit, and they would get all straightened up with their best hat on properly, and then they'd start yawning again.

By this we could see they weren't sports, like they wanted the world to think they were. They were just boys who had jobs where they had to get up early in the morning and go off in the streetcars to their factories or wherever it was they were working before the sun had came up. Just about the time I'd be getting in from playing somewheres they'd be starting to go to work. Half the time they'd start to go to sleep before they had a chance to drink everything they'd paid all that money for, and the glass would sit there in front of them until one of the girls who worked in the place would take it away and tell them they had to buy another one.

You can understand by this that Mildred looked very good to the boys in the boarding house, but the truth was Mildred wasn't interested in anybody but me. Now since I was new to the town I didn't have anything else lined up and when she wasn't so busy telling you what a high class lady she was Mildred wasn't so bad. As I said she was very pretty, and if she thought nobody was looking at her then she would get down off her high seat and she'd begin to laugh a little. Of course it wouldn't last very long, because she couldn't let you think she was just a plain girl from out in the country somewhere, but you could get the feeling that she wasn't so awful all the way through. So one night when I got through playing I came back to the boarding house a little early. I didn't stay out and have myself some breakfast the way I was used to doing. I came up the stairs very quietly so as not to arouse anybody and instead of going to my room I went down the little hall to where Mildred had her room. Of course I knew I would have to have some excuse before she would let me come in, but I had my story ready for her when I knocked. Now she must have been lying there wondering if I might come, because there wasn't time for a cat to jump across the room after a mouse

114

before she was at the door.

She didn't open it right away. I could hear her standing on the other side of it catching her breath and I think she was probably getting her hair all straight and maybe she put on something over her nightgown. But after a minute she said in a very low voice, who is it, and I told her and she said it was too late in the night for me to come knocking at her door. Then I gave her my little story about how somebody had gone through my pocket when I was changing my clothes at the club and they had taken my key, and I was locked out of my room. Now I knew Mildred had a key to open the door to every room which she had to check up on some of those boys if they were thinking of leaving without paying up and their suitcases weren't in the room where they should have been.

Anyway, she pretended like she was thinking about what I had told her, then after a minute she opened the door and stepped out of the way so I wouldn't come too close to her when I picked up the key, which she had over on her dressing table, but I think she just wanted to take a step or two backwards so I could look her over. Now Mildred had looked very good to me when she was all dressed up, but when she had on just her nightgown and a little robe made out of silk she had pulled over it she looked like one of those beautiful girls who worked with me on the shows. They would pose on the stage for "living pictures," as they called them, and we would give them some kind of name like "The Bronze Goddess." She had the looks to get a job like that anytime she wanted. I'm telling you, that figure of hers was enough to make a man cry. There I was, inside the

115

door, in my best suit of clothes and I still had on my hat, but I had pushed it back on my head the way a sport does when he's at a baseball game, and I could see that I looked as good to her as she did to me. So I went on talking about the place where I had been playing and all the people who had came to the place to hear my music and so forth and so on, and all the time I was trying to think of some way to get her to close the door. It was very important for Mildred that everything had to be done in a very proper way.

Now, as I said, I always carried with me a large roll of money so if anybody tried to bluff me in any sort of game I was ready for him and the idea came to me that Mildred was the type of woman who would like to look at some money. So I said in a low voice, you don't know what kind of money a guy like me makes on a job when there's plenty people listening and giving you tips for their request numbers. Of course she got very interested when I said money, but she came back at me, what you talking about, what kind of money. It's just one kind of money that I ever heard of. What is this special kind that you got?

That kind of stumped me on account of I had just came in from the street, but I said back at her after a minute had gone by, sweetheart, I got dollar bills here that go so high up in their numbers that they don't just print the President's head on it. They got his whole body standing there in a new suit of clothes. And she started to laugh, but all the time she was keeping her voice low so nobody could hear us, so I knew I was going to get there. Very slowly, so as to keep her looking at what I was doing, I pulled the roll of bills out of my pocket with one hand and with the other hand I started to ease the door closed.

She gave me one of those looks, you know, with her lips all pushed out like she was sulky, and she said, what you doing with the door? And I said in a very low voice, even though I always carry a pistol it wouldn't be safe if anybody saw all this money that I'm carrying around with me. Now there wasn't a person in the whole place who wasn't sleeping, and they couldn't see down the hall where her room was anyway, but I tried to look very serious and Mildred thought about it for a minute and she let me close the door so nobody could see the money. Of course after that when I had taken the roll of bills out of my pocket so she could see it was real, she wanted to hold on to it. I held it up above my head so she'd have to stand beside me to reach up for it and in a minute she stopped worrying about what people thought of her.

I must have stayed with Mildred for two or three months and I hate to say it, but at the beginning Mildred didn't have any more idea what she was doing than a mule would dancing the Bunny Hop. I'm telling you that first night it was like I had taken a pillow in my arms and fallen head foremost down a flight of stairs. I don't know who she started off with in Mississippi, but that fellow, I swear, didn't know which end he was working on. Now I had known so many women from the shows and so forth and of course some of the real sweet girls in the houses when the customers had gone home and I didn't have to stay seated at the piano. If it had been in New Orleans or Los Angeles where I knew somebody else I would have gotten up and gotten out of there, but since I was new in town I said to myself, you're going to have to teach Mildred some things, which I then taken it upon myself to do. Now this made such a hit with Mildred that she couldn't get enough of me. She tried to keep it hid when people had came into the dining room for meals, but I could see some of the boys looking at her, and they had an idea something was happening. This made Mildred decide we had to get away sometimes so she went out one day and bought herself a brand new Marmon automobile and she came back and gave me the keys. That was what a simple woman like that would do if she wanted to keep a man with her. So she would put on her best dress and I would get into one of my good suits and I would go out first and get the car ready and after a minute she would come walking around the corner and she would get in and we would go driving in the car.

Now, once Mildred had learned a few things she wasn't so bad and I was getting the best things at the table when it was time for dinner so I said to myself, you got it pretty good, and for a time Mildred and I got very close to each other. But the other side of Mildred, putting on a front and making herself out to be so special and knowing everything because she owned a boarding house and she had been in Chicago for almost four years, that got worse than ever. Having me around made her think she was even more special and she was always after me to take her to some fancy places so people could see she was with a man who had snappy clothes and was very light in complexion. Some of the people who had came to Chicago didn't think anything about where they had come from. If you asked them they said whatever it was, even if it was just some little bitty place nobody ever heard of down in Tennessee. But for Mildred being from that town in Mississippi, if it was even a town it was so small, she thought that was the tragedy of her life, and that was to be the cause of the trouble between us.

She knew sometimes I went out with people I had known from California or New Orleans and we would have little parties when we got through with our jobs and she begged to be taken out when I went on one of these parties. So the next time it was to be a party for one of the guys I told her, alright, you can come along, but I don't want you to do any dancing or anything like that to cause you to draw attention to yourself. I didn't really want to take Mildred with me because I mostly was hanging out with Creole fellows and they didn't like to have anything to do with women who had a dark complexion. They thought it would bring them down, in a manner of speaking. But Mildred was giving me the best of everything at the boarding house and she had made me a present of the keys to that Marmon automobile so I thought I would let her come along with me.

Now I was beginning to make good money so I said to her that she should come with me to the store because I didn't know her sizes, and I would pick out something for her to put on. I took her to the best clothing store in Chicago and said she should take whatever she wanted. Of course once we got inside the door poor Mildred got so nervous she couldn't open up her mouth and even with that very good figure and her hair fixed very nice and a new coat with a fox fur collar she still looked like somebody who had just came out of Mississippi, so it was necessary for me to tell the lady what we wanted. I decided that what Mildred needed was a blue dress

119

that was cut a little jagged around the bottom and had lots of beads on it. Mildred was very pleased with it and I could see she felt this was very important that I had bought her a dress, but all I was thinking about was that I didn't want those boys to think I was being nice to somebody who didn't have any class at all.

Now, when the time for the party came we got in the car and went off to a restaurant down on the lake and when we got there everybody was gathered and even though it was against the law of course, some of the fellows had gotten everything in the way of drinks and everybody was laughing and amusing themselves. We had taken over a room by ourselves and it had a piano and a place to dance and there was a kind of balcony that went out to the lake over the water. For a time Mildred did alright. Nobody had anything to say to her and she was too afraid to say anything to them so she sat beside me in that blue beaded dress and just looked at everybody. Of course she was drinking at the same time which was intended to keep her from feeling so nervous. There were four or five other women at the party, but they were from New Orleans and they weren't any of them as dark as Mildred, so they didn't give her more than a look. Now I had so much more experience of the world I could see what was going to happen, but every time I would try and take the glass from Mildred's hand she would take another drink. The later it got, the worse she was, but she still wasn't talking and she sat in the same chair the whole time while I went off and met everybody who had come there. I think everything still would have been alright, because as long as she didn't do anything but sit there she looked good enough and everybody thought she must have some idea about clothes because of the dress I had selected for her.

Mildred's downfall was caused by one of the boys starting on the piano. They had asked me if I would be willing to play for them, but I said I was only there to say hello, so this other fellow asked me if it was alright if he sat down on the piano stool. He had to ask me because he knew I could beat him at anything he might play, but I thought to myself, hell, everybody in the place knows I can beat him so it doesn't matter what he wants to do. You understand, the place wasn't the most elegant you could find. Some of those white places where I was playing were very elegant, with all kinds of mirrors and tables covered with pure white linen and silver spoons and forks and so forth and so on. The places where Negroes could go weren't so fine, and although some of the fellows and the girls they had brought with them could have passed, Negroes was what we were considered to be. But the people who owned the restaurant had tried to make it look as nice as they could and there was streamers all around the piano and they had paper lanterns over the lights that hung down from the ceiling.

Now when the fellow started in at the piano people got up and started in to dancing and it was all very proper and classy and everybody was no doubt satisfied at the time they were having. But once the dancing started I could see Mildred was too far gone to know what she was doing. She started doing little jumps with her legs and she twisted around in her chair and then she'd start in to laughing. That was the way they did it in those country places, and I won't say they don't have a lot of pleasure in that kind of behavior, but there's always things you have to give up if you want to come a little higher and that's what those country people didn't want to learn.

Now, the fellow at the piano could see her wringing and twisting there on the chair and he had been drinking and he wasn't in much better shape than she was. Between the two of them I don't think they could have told you the difference between a monkey and a giraffe if the giraffe leaned down to take a sip out of their glasses. The fellow was forgetting I was right there and if he started something with her he was going to have to get me out of the way, but he kept on playing these kind of numbers that made her jump around on that chair. All those barrel house numbers, very low class. Now the other people could see what he was doing and when they looked at me to see if I was on to him and I just laughed then they went along with it. It was sad to see it, because in a way they weren't doing nothing except laughing at her.

The fellow got so carried away he started playing one of those new Charleston numbers with that little break in the rhythm. Now there was not one person in the city of Chicago who could play that kind of tune in the correct tempo except myself, but he could do something that sounded a little bit like it and that was good enough for Mildred. She jumped up and started kicking her legs up the way they do the Charleston out in the country and everybody got out of her way because she couldn't keep her balance too good and she was waving her arms around. The wilder she got in her dancing the hotter that fellow got at the piano and finally it was just the two of them having their own party. She was perspiring so all her make-up was getting runny and the process was coming out of her hair and she was getting all wild-looking. Then she taken it into her mind to do the high kicks. Now this was the dance only the lowest class of women did in those honky tonks down South. She was dancing with her head back and she could see the paper lantern on the light which was hanging down over the dance floor, and she decided she would kick the lantern off the light. Now she kept on dancing all the time, but every now and then she'd kick as high as she could at the light and the little Japanese paper latern that was covering it. Some of the fellows were encouraging her to keep kicking and they were looking at her legs and they were laughing so loud you hardly could hear the music.

Of course the other women weren't laughing at all and they were making the fellows with them look in some other direction. Finally one of those fellows stood up and walked over to the piano and with one hand he took hold of the wrist of the boy who was playing the Charleston number and with his other hand he slammed down the cover over the keys of the piano. He slammed it down so hard it sounded like a pistol going off and everybody got very still. Then the fellow looked over at me and he said in a loud voice, Jelly Roll, you could have told us you were planning to bring a nigger to our party.

Now Mildred was still standing in the middle of the room trying to catch her breath and when the fellow said that she started crying and she turned around and ran out the door. Now the club was built right over the lake in the style they had then and there was a porch where you could walk around and look out across the water. The next thing we heard was a

123

splash. Mildred had fallen over the porch railing into the lake. Two or three of the fellows had to climb down the supports they had there to hold the porch up and pull her out of the water before she drowned.

Of course, after that there was no way Mildred could look me in the face again. We carried her out to the car with her dress all soaking wet and torn up the side and her hair sticking out like she was some kind of porcupine and we put her in the back seat and she just lay there moaning. By the time I had gotten the car back to the boarding house she was passed out and I was in a little trouble because she was too heavy for me to carry her out by myself, and I didn't think it was right for me to wake up some of the boys in the boarding house to get help. If the boys she had staying there lost respect for her it could be very hard for her to do business with them. So what I did was taken her to a corner where I knew some of those whores did their business and when one of them came over to look into the window of the car to let me know she was available I showed her Mildred and said I would pay her a dollar if she would help me to carry Mildred up her steps. When she had taken a look she took to laughing and she told two or three of the other girls to come look. I'm telling you, if Mildred had woken up at that moment and seen those street women looking in the window of the car and laughing at her she would have died right then and there. But the woman asked me if I didn't want more than just some help getting Mildred into her bed and I said, no, I had ten minutes to get the job taken care of and all I was going to pay was a dollar, so the woman just got in the car and between the two of us pushing and pulling we got Mildred up to her room.

Now the next morning she never showed up in the dining room and the cook and the maid had to take care of everything for themselves. I understood it would be better if I didn't hang around so I taken my things and found another boarding house across town. The only question that was worrying me was what I should do about the keys to the car which she had presented to me and I knew there would be trouble if I didn't take care of the keys in a proper manner, so I hung them on her doorknob where she would find them when she came out of her room. I saw her one more time about a week later when I was walking along the street close to where she had her boarding house and she was walking along the sidewalk, but she turned her face the other way and wouldn't even look at me. I felt sorry for her, but I knew it wouldn't do any good for me to go up to her and start talking. They had some sorry times, people like Mildred. There was all those things they had to learn about, and they didn't have anybody who could help them.

From that time on in Chicago my life was strictly music, and one reason that came about was that I had became so famous I couldn't hustle the boys at pool the way I was used to doing. I would go around for a friendly game, you know trying to set up some sucker so he would bet against me and then I would run the table and take his money, but people would look at me when I came in the joint and as soon as I would start to talk about putting a little money on the next ball the fellow, my sucker, he'd say, Jelly Roll, here's a quarter for the next game, why don't you find somebody else to play with you. You see, he knew I was a shark. It wasn't like those old days in St. Louis or Houston or some place like that where nobody knew who I was. Now everybody in the country knew who I was. I don't think there was a person living in the United States of America who hadn't heard of me unless he happened to be deaf and dumb.

On their advertisements the Victor Company called me the No. 1 Hot Band in the Country, and everywhere you'd go people would be buying my records. This had come about on account of the arrangements I had made of my own tunes and put down on records with some of the boys I had known from New Orleans as well as some other boys I had met up in Chicago. Ory was in town from California and Johnny Lindsay and St. Cyr had came up from New Orleans and they knew the kind of rhythm I was looking for. I had given a chance to that light-skinned boy Simeon who was just starting out to play clarinet and he learned so many things from working with me that he later went to the top. Now the fellow I used on cornet, George Mitchell, he was from Kentucky, which meant he didn't know how to play as free as those boys from New Orleans, but if you told him to be some place at nine o'clock he'd be there right on time and there was never any kind of trouble with drinking or arguing with you like you had with those

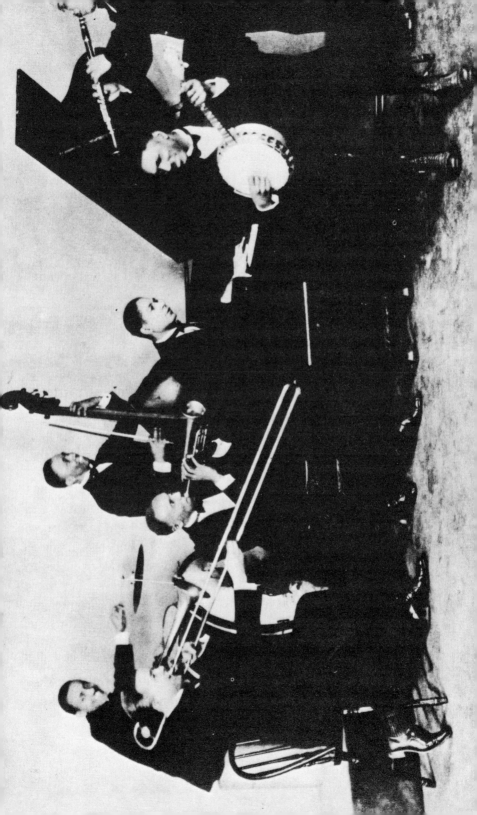

other fellows.

Now I had been famous all my life and people had recognized me to be the foremost piano player in the country and I had made some records before, but the contract with the Victor Company was my chance to spread my music everywhere people listened to records, which was everywhere in the world. The fact of the matter is none of the jazz records which had been made before that time came up to what the standard of jazz music could be, and I was the one who changed all that. When I had taken the opportunity to make those records for those other companies I had been learning how to do things better. You can listen to all those other fellows who were making records at the same time, Duke Ellington and King Oliver and Fletcher Henderson and all of them, which have became famous names, and I was ahead of them all. The fact of the matter is they were able to get ahead by listening to what I was putting down on record.

The way I made those boys play the way I wanted was by my writing down in notes all the parts of the arrangements and then they came to the apartment I had taken after I had left the last boarding house and we rehearsed until everything was right. Of course Mitchell, the fellow who was on cornet, he wasn't so good with his solos so I had to write down notes to help him out, but with the other fellows I let them make their own solos so long as they fit into my arrangement. Then when we went to the studio to put down the tunes we had everything right, and I wouldn't let the fellows drink too much so they played in tune and they read the notes the way they were supposed to. Now you take Ory, he could drink like a mule coming back to the barn after a day hauling a wagon in the hot sun, and you listen to those records he was making with Louis Armstrong at the same time as he was working with me and it makes you want to laugh at the noises he was making because Louis was letting him drink. I kept them all to the music and that's why we came out so far ahead of everybody else.

Now those people who go around saying, all Jelly can do is talk, all they have to do is listen to those records. When you're traveling around the country like I was doing in my early days you have to listen to every kind of music in order to know what the public wants. I believe every kind of music which I heard about is no doubt in those arrangements somewhere. I know you have heard the records yourself and you know what I'm talking about. The vaudeville parts, which I had taken from all the shows, that comes out in those numbers like "Sidewalk Blues" or "Steamboat Stomp," and the blues parts comes out in "Smokehouse Blues" and "Cannonball Blues," only I changed the harmonies to be all my own way and not just those kiddy chords everybody else was using. Of course in "Deadman Blues" I put in all the kinds of music from New Orleans and my specialty number, "Jelly Roll Blues," had a chorus which was played with a tango rhythm and that was something else we had in New Orleans in those days. As fast as those records hit the market, they sold out and everywhere you went people were trying to play my tunes and my arrangements. I'm telling you if I had a dollar for every time I have heard a band mess up one of my numbers I wouldn't be sitting up there on the piano stool. I'd have two more Cadillacs and another hundred suits of clothes and I'd pay somebody else to play the piano for me.

Of course now I was so famous I could go out on tours and do appearances anytime I wanted but another thing about Chicago which caused me to stay strictly with music was that you couldn't do anything in the line of girls or introducing people to some place where they could have a good time or some of those other things my partners and I had been doing in Los Angeles. Everything in Chicago was done by the mobs, and even though I always carried with me the pistol I had inside my coat pocket, I knew they would kill me in a minute if I started anything along the lines they had an interest in. I was making so much money just taking an orchestra around to play for people who were buying my records I didn't need to think about those things, but the fact of the matter is the way things are going today I can't help thinking sometimes about all those things I had going for me back then. If you have a talent for something then you just naturally have to go along with that talent, which is what I've done all my life, even if it was a talent for things not pertaining to music.

But even if some things change in your life, you don't stop being yourself. I hadn't been in Chicago more than two or three years when it began to feel small to me. The mob was in charge of all the night clubs on account of the prohibition and if they taken a dislike to somebody then they would just freeze him out or do worser things like leaving him down in the bottom of Lake Michigan with cement about his ankles. I had seen so many tougher guys in New Orleans I wasn't afraid of what they could do to me, but if you had a band, the club had to give them a little money for protection and so forth and so on and they would tell you where you had to take your clothes for the band to get them cleaned, and all the things in that line.

Now I had been moving around too free to let them put me in that situation since they weren't nothing but a bunch of dagos in the first place. So I decided to go to New York, not knowing that the situation was the same thing there and they owned everything and if you wanted to take your orchestra into some place like the Cotton Club then you had to do whatever the gangsters told you to do. The places that stayed open all was run by the gangs that brought in the liquor and if there was a dispute about which mob was going to bring in the liquor then there would be a little bit of an explosion and instead of a night club there would just be a pile of boards and some bricks. Now a lot of the boys didn't mind playing for the mobs. The reason for that was the dagos didn't care so much what color anybody was. They didn't give a damn if the orchestra up on the stage was black or white or yellow just so they could play and the people would be satisfied with them. Of course if the boys didn't want to work for those class of men they would get into trouble and this happened to two or three lovely clubs in Harlem that had the idea they would go into competition with the Cotton Club. They had to close their doors. So the fellows in the orchestras went along with it and they made pretty good money.

It was just about this time, when I was getting ready to leave Chicago and go to New York, that I met Mabel Bertrand, the lady who was to become Mrs. Morton. Of course I didn't know that when I first saw her. She was working in a cabaret there in Chicago, singing and dancing, and I had known so many women in the shows and working in the cabarets that I didn't think there was any chance for me getting tangled up with that kind of woman. She hadn't been working that type of job for very long. I could tell that from the way she held herself when she was performing. She didn't have that natural look. But she could entertain the people and she was young and she was very pretty. Everybody in the place knew who I was and I had on a suit of clothes which had just been made for me by one of the finest establishments in Chicago and she could see the diamonds shining on my tie and my fingers and on my teeth so she was very willing to come sit down at my table when it was time to take a break. Now when we commenced to talking the surprise was on me because she wasn't at all the kind of girl I thought she was.

She wouldn't promise to meet me, and when I made her an offer of money, as is only natural when you meet a woman under those circumstances, she got very hot with me. She was another one of those high-class Creole women from New Orleans, like Anita Gonzales. Her family was in the very best society circles down in New Orleans and that was one thing that attracted me to her. Like all those girls she

132

could drive you almost crazy reminding you about this or that and always fussing at you to do something they wanted you to do for them. You no doubt have heard the tune I wrote for her, "Fussy Mabel." She wasn't so pleased to have a song like that with her name on it, but when she heard how pretty it was she stopped fussing with me over it.

It was after that I began to drop by the cabaret where she was working almost every night and she certainly knew how to use those Creole ways. But it didn't make any difference how many times I asked her to come out with me or told her how I would give her a beautiful present if she'd come for a ride with me, she just pursed out her lips and put her chin up and said she wasn't interested. She only wanted one thing from me and that was a ring. So I got to thinking about it and I was planning to go to New York and I had the opportunity to take her with me, so finally she agreed to come with me in my new Cadillac automobile, but she only agreed to come with me to one place, and that was to the little place over the state line in Indiana where you had to go if you wanted to get married in a hurry.

So Mabel and I got married and then I packed up all of our things in the Cadillac and we moved to New York where I found us a very elegant apartment in Harlem just off Seventh Avenue on 131st Street. I moved in the best furniture money could buy and I bought a grand piano so I would have the opportunity to compose my new tunes and arrangements any time an idea came to me. I was never the kind of person to change what I was doing without a very good reason. When you have been conducting your business one way all your life and you find that your way of doing this is successful, then the only thing for you to do is to continue the way which you have commenced. I was used to doing everything one way. My way. And I had the proof that I was on to the right way which was my records for the Victor Company. I had no sooner gotten to New York than I picked up a new bunch of boys and made some new records that were a bigger success than what I had been doing in Chicago. That was those numbers of mine like "Georgia Swing" and "Kansas City Stomps" and "Mournful Serenade." The fellows was all new to my music, except for Simeon, who was in New York, and he had made those numbers with me when he was just starting out, so I asked him if he wanted a chance to do something with me again. What I did which made it so successful was writing down the notes to the arrangements just the way I wanted those fellows to play them. And we had our rehearsals until we got it right and that made all the difference.

Sometimes people will tell you Jelly was hard on the boys he had working for him. I know you must have heard somebody say that. The fact of the matter is I never was hard on anybody when I had those top musicians from New Orleans working in my bands. But I couldn't take them out on the road with me because the people who owned the clubs where they were working wouldn't allow them to leave town. We would have those rehearsals to get everything the way we wanted and then we would make the records and then I'd sign a contract to play at theaters and clubs and dance halls everywhere around those towns outside of New York and up to Massachusetts and Buffalo and Cleveland and I would have to get a whole new bunch of boys to take out on the road with me. Now when they were working with me they had come to the top because I was the No. 1 Hot Band for the Victor Company and I could get any job I wanted, but this might have made them kind of jealous and I'd hear them saying things behind my back. Then we'd come to some little bitty place to play a dance and one of the fellows would tell me he wanted to go back home. Go back and suck on your mother's tit, I'd tell him, and then we'd have an argument and I'd have to find somebody else to work in his place.

I never did understand why those boys would want to leave. As long as they stayed with me they were with the man who had invented jazz. They were up there on the bandstand with the man who knew more about how jazz music was supposed to be played than anybody else in the world. But for some reason I never did understand they would get salty with me if they couldn't get the arrangements right and I would tell them they didn't know how to play their instrument and they didn't know anything about music. When I taken a man out in front of the band and told him that the truth was he couldn't play at all, he should have been glad somebody told him so he could go out and get an honest job for himself and quit trying to fool everybody by saying he was a musician. Now I know after they left me sometimes the fellow would go over to Duke Ellington or Fletcher Henderson or Cab Calloway and get a job, but he was lucky because in those bands nobody knew enough about music to notice if he could play or not. I hate to say a thing like this, but the fact is, if he did good after he left me it was only because of all

135

the things I had taught him.

It was at that time that I invented a little scheme to keep my eye on the boys when I was sitting down at the piano and I know somebody must have said to you, Jelly had eyes in the back of his head. I knew some of them would be cutting up because they would be jealous of me as I was so well known everywhere we went, and they would take to laughing and making faces in the middle of an arrangement. To do something about this I had taken a piece of a mirror and slipped it in between the pieces of music I carried up to the piano with me, and then I would slide out that mirror so I would see what was happening behind me and if I'd see maybe the trumpet player puffing out his cheeks or sitting there with his foot up on his leg then I'd jump up and turn around and I'd say, right there, boy, you've got your two. This meant I was giving him two weeks notice so he could start to think about another job. I know this wasn't popular with some of them but it was all things they had to learn if they wanted to get ahead in the music business.

I have to tell a story on myself. Sometimes when you're new to a town you don't know everything that's going on and you can make a mistake which can cause you a lot of trouble. I was about to go on the road again and I was rehearsing the arrangements I had written of some of my new tunes and we had a little trouble to find a drummer and finally one of the other boys brought in this new fellow. His name was Wright, and the name didn't mean anything to me.

When we had commenced rehearsing one of the tunes this fellow Wright started playing all out of time and coming in wrong and I walked over to him and I said, I hope you got yourself a good job on the side doing something like folding up paper bags because you sure as hell can't play the drums. He looked up at me very slowly and then he said, you open your mouth one more time and I'm going to whip you around so fast you'll think a streetcar ran over you. Now I never was afraid of anybody because I always had my pistol in my coat pocket, but of course it was a hot day and I had taken the coat off and it was on the other side of the room. But I looked down at him and I said to him, you think you're so tough. Who'd you ever kill? And the place got all quiet. I had the feeling everybody there but me was holding their breath. This fellow Wright smiled back at me and he said in a soft voice, "Jim Europe." And then the place got so quiet, if somebody had dropped a feather to the floor it would have sounded like a clap of thunder.

I found out later that what he said was the truth. The famous Jim Europe, the first Negro to lead an orchestra in the best cabarets and night spots in New York City, the leader of General Pershing's brass band that played for the soldiers over in France, had been stabbed to death in his dressing room by this fellow Herbert Wright. But I didn't know that. The other boys let me find it out for myself.

There was so much in the line of music and entertaining up in Harlem when I came there with Mrs. Morton, I'm telling you. Since the police had

137

closed down the district in Storyville back during the war I don't suppose there was any place on the face of the globe with as much going on in it as Harlem in those days. Of course I had no trouble when I went out looking for a job and before you could bat an eye I had an orchestra composed of some of the finest musicians in New York City and I had a contract at Rose's Danceland, which was at the corner of Seventh Avenue and 125th Street. Now it was a job which had hard hours, but I was used to that from all the places I had worked all my life, and some of the boys I had with me understood my music and we got along very well. Ward Pinkett, the fellow I had playing trumpet with me, was a very nice kind of a guy and sometimes we would meet and go out to eat at a restaurant, some of that cooking from down South, and we would tell all kinds of jokes together. Russell Procope, who was playing the sax and clarinet, and the two Benford brothers, Tommy and Bill, they all was nice guys and they worked those hours without ever getting down on me.

It was what you call a "taxi dance hall," which means that they had girls there who would dance with anyone who came in the door in exchange for a ticket which he would buy from the booth they had set up where you entered. Of course that meant they didn't want us to play pieces which went on too long. Every time we stopped the customer had to hand over another one of his tickets to the girl. And of course they didn't want us to stop playing, which would mean there was nothing for the girls to do except hang around the railing that was set up for them there to wait for the men, and they'd try to get one of the customers to buy them a drink. Now the girls had to keep going to make any kind of money and some of them were known never to go to the toilet all night. If somebody would buy them a drink they would just sip at it and when he wasn't looking they would pour it out. And they would still be dancing when the customers would all be worn out and looking for a taxi to take them home.

I never would take a drink myself in those days, which would make it possible for me to be always ready with anything the customers wanted. You see me drinking a little whiskey now, but of course I take a drink every now and then, and this is the last night here. When I am home with Mrs. Morton I don't drink anything more than a little sherry. Sherry wine. You no doubt have heard the song I sing about that, which I learned from Tony Jackson so many years ago. Water in Michigan tastes like sherry wine. I never knew why Tony was so particular that it was the water in Michigan that tasted so good, just like I never understand why the Spikes Brothers made my tune up into something about Michigan, on account of Michigan being known for wolverines. I never could make a damn nickle in Detroit and the rest of the place didn't look to me to be nothing but trees.

You might have noticed that I have this cough that sometimes gives me a little trouble. It's nothing more than the weather around here and it will go away as soon as I have gotten back to someplace warm. Of course I get a little tired talking, but you been so good listening I want to get to the end of the story.

Some of the jobs I had with Pinkett and those guys were a lot easier and after we made some more records for the Victor company we had people wanting us everywhere around and I got us a bus and we would set out to play all those dances and shows. The trouble was, as I told you, I couldn't keep the same guys and I'd have to be firing the fellows that was getting smart and somebody would tell me he had to go home and I was forced to look for somebody new when I was out on the road, which is very hard to keep up the standard. Very hard. I would think sometimes how much more simpler it had been when I was just a piano player and a pool shark and I could go into any town in the country and play me up some meals and I could make enough money in one night playing pool so I could lay around until I got in the notion to go on to the next town. I was always worrying about whether the boys wasn't drinking too much and was somebody counting how many customers had came in the door so I wasn't being cheated on the money and did somebody put gas in the bus so we could get going the next morning and was the hotel alright for me to sleep in with my wife. The times had changed for fellows like me who had came up in a different time. Now we had our chance to make our big break and it seemed everything had changed up on us. Sometimes I would get so hot with the type of fellows I had to work for me I would fire them all and then I wouldn't have to worry myself about all those things.

Then it would be quiet for a time, let me tell you. I would sit every day at my grand piano and I would compose tunes and write arrangements so I would be ready for the next thing that came down the road. And I decided to go into the music business again, as I had done in Los Angeles, which I did taking a

partner who I won't name for fear he would bring a lawsuit against me for anything I might say about him. I'm telling you. That fellow knew tricks that would have made a magician look like he was just a beginner. We had set us up in a music publishing company and we had an office so we could do business, but it got so bad with that fellow I had to take all the tunes which I had in partnership with him and sell them to somebody else to get my money back out of the deal and this fellow turned around and caused me to have trouble with the fellows I had sold the songs to. I think sometimes that the fellow that invented all those business kind of arrangements did it just to catch up on all of us who had genuine talent, because when everything is all over with it's the business people who have all the money and what we get out of it is a letter telling us we have violated the terms of their contracts. I'm telling you it's a crime what happens to somebody who tries to do something on his own. There's no man living can do what I can do on the piano, but there's fellows out there who are making more money at it when they can't play at all.

Another thing which made so many changes was the orchestra getting so much larger so that little effects I was used to putting in my music didn't go over in the same manner. Now when I had a small band every instrument was like one of my own fingers and everybody knows what I can do with my fingers when it comes down to music. What I wrote in my arrangements came directly from what I had played on the piano myself. Now they wanted you to have so many men in the orchestra you'd get the feeling when you were doing an arrangement that you had run out of fingers.

It didn't take me any time to learn the new little tricks they had in the music and of course everything came out in my style, so I was ready to go ahead and I had my tunes all ready. But then the business part of it started going bad, only this time I didn't have anything to do with it. It was the white people's business that started to go bad. If it hadn't been so hard for so many people there was Negroes who was ready to laugh about the whole thing. The white people all the time telling us that we never will learn how to run things for ourselves and we always going to need them to take care of us, and then along comes 1929 and they can't do it any better. I'm telling you some of the boys said right at the start that it all had commenced because those white fellows couldn't stand to see us get a little ahead, which was beginning to happen, and they had the idea if they could make things go bad for a little while then they would get us down at the bottom again. And right at the beginning it looked like that was the way it was because we lost our jobs first and the people who was buying my records they didn't have the money to buy nothing with. But then we could see the same thing happening to them and it was understood that everything they had tried was like a man who is setting out to put a sack over a snake but he's got his eyes blindfolded. They didn't know what the hell they were doing.

The fact of the matter is sometimes when I begin to go over in my mind so many of the things which have happened to me I think I have came into one of those funny rooms like they have at a carnival. I know you have experienced them just as I have. Everywhere on the wall are all kind of mirrors and you look at

143

yourself in one and your legs are all long and wavy and you start in to laughing and then the next one your face is all the way down to the floor and you feel very sad. All those things anybody remembers are just like that and they no doubt can laugh or cry when they see some of the places they have been and what they have done. That may sound a little strange, but when you are a little older you'll have a better idea of what I'm talking about.

When times got hard back there in twenty-nine and thirty I don't think there was a person around who would have said it would stay hard. Of course I always had the ability to make something go together for myself and with my name being so well known from my tunes and my records I always could find the people which had the money to get behind me. And that's what I'm waiting for now, and I have everything ready for them. Now that situation I was mentioning to you, about feeling that I had came into some kind of a room filled with mirrors when I started to think back to the old times. That was what I experienced after a while at the club here. It isn't much of a place when you come to consider some of the type of places I have played in before this, but there was no time of the day or night when you wouldn't find entertainment or music to please you. We had so many artists waiting to present their talent and of course I was the master of ceremonies and I filled in at the piano. I also did some of the cooking. When people wanted that New Orleans style cooking they had came to the right place because I had grown up eating that way. Now that was the time those fellows started coming in to ask me about those days in New Orleans and who I had known and who I had

144

played with and had I heard some of the old fellows like Buddy Bolden and so forth and so on.

Now that had taken me a little by surprise because all these fellows were white and I didn't think there was anybody white who had any idea what kind of music we had been making all those years, and they were young. I'm telling you, they were so young I was worried about letting them come into a place where liquor was being served. Perhaps you are acquainted with some of those gentlemen? Of course when I say "young" I'm not talking about Mr. Carew, who used to hang around when we had the battles of music in Storyville. He has kindly taken a hand with my music copyrights to protect me against some of those crooks hanging around out there. But maybe you met Mr. Lomax, Alan Lomax, who is with the Library of Congress, and Charles Smith, and Bill Russell and Fred Ramsey? The truth is, when they first started asking me all these things I didn't understand what it was they wanted. I was all set to go ahead, and what they wanted was for me to go back. It took me a little time to learn what was happening, which was that I had to go backwards if I wanted to go forwards. But then I learned it. It was about the same time I got into that argument with Handy, W. C. Handy out of Memphis who had put his name on the "St. Louis Blues," about who had started jazz music. That got wrote up in all the newspapers and led to me appearing on NBC radio and playing my old numbers, and after that the Victor Company got interested in me again.

Of course, when those fellows came in to talk to me about the old days I wasn't the only person they were interested in. It seemed like they wanted to come into contact with anyone from those times, and they kept asking me did I know this fellow or what had happened to that one. The fact of the matter is I knew all them boys from New Orleans and I was able to put those fellows into contact with so many of them who were still living. And you no doubt have heard the records which I made for the new companies these fellows found for me and all those sides which I have made for the Library of Congress. It was for the Library that I gave them everything they ever would need to know about how jazz started and the fellow who was asking the questions, Alan Lomax, had came to know so many things nobody had ever heard of before we were through. Afterwards it was Smith, Charles Smith, who came up to New York and was in charge of the records I made about my New Orleans memories. I was staying with Mrs. Morton again after we had been apart while I took care of the club down there in Washington, and he would come up there to Harlem and listen to me play on the grand piano and we would decide what we wanted to do and then we would have a supper of red beans and rice or New Orleans style shrimp.

I still thought it was very strange that what they wanted from me was all those things from so long ago, but I always was accustomed to giving the customer what he requested and it was natural for me to follow their wishes. Being around those fellows, in a manner of speaking, was the cause of taking me back so many years. If I didn't know better I would say it's a sign that I was getting old. All these people wanting to know what I used to do instead of what I was going to do next, but the fact is they also helped me to go forward, and they brought my name back before the public, and now that I have another chance I can go forward anyway that satisfies me.

I can see it's getting very late and I should be getting ready to pack up everything so I can start on my way. As I already told you some things haven't changed at all and that's how I know I'm not old yet. The places I've been living now, New York and Washington, they're beginning to feel small to me, just like always. So tomorrow morning I'll be on my way. When you're thinking of going someplace you say you're bound there. So I'm Hollywood bound. Of course I have some business to take care of in New York, and I have to pack up all my suits and all my music which is there on the grand piano on 133rd Street, but it's Hollywood that's in my mind while I'm sitting here talking to you. I could hang around here and let people hear my new numbers and so forth and so on, but the time comes when you have to move on. My godmother who was living out in Los Angeles has been taken sick and died and she had certain of my property I have to attend to, and my wife has expressed her wishes to return to New Orleans until I get everything set up in the finest way for her to come and the doctors have told me all that sunshine out there will take care of my cough. So like they say in the blues, I'm booked out and bound to go.

147

But I won't go crawling out to Hollywood. I'm going to take my two automobiles, the Lincoln and the Cadillac, and I'm going to fill one of them with my suits and I'm going to hitch them together, one right behind the other, and I'm going to take them with me out to Hollywood. I have had so many letters from my fans out there who have heard me on my radio broadcasts and that has made them excited waiting for me to come out in person and show them what I can do. If you've got a talent which God has gave to you it don't do any good to try to hide it because people will come looking for you. You can put your light down under a bushel basket, but little rays from that light are going to come shining through for everybody to see. And while I am satisfying my fans this will give me the opportunity to take care of that business about my godmother.

I have had so many people tell me to my face, Jelly, you all washed up. You get on out of here with that old time stuff. Now I know my style is not behind the times because right now any time you turn on the radio you hear the great hot orchestras playing my numbers and you hear them trying to execute my ideas. I never did pay any attention when somebody would try to run me down like that because I knew what it was I had. If you want jazz music you have to come to me because this is the only place you can get it. In a manner of speaking you might say that I am the well water that all those other fellows are drinking from, and they don't even know it.

I see you haven't finished your drink, and we never did do much damage to this bottle the boy brought over for us from the bar. When you get to talking you don't think about other things. As I told you

148

before, when you start telling stories like this about your early days and what you have done and people you have known and so forth and so on, it's almost like you're explaining yourself and explaining about what your life has been like. When we have another chance to spend an evening and you tell me some of your stories you will no doubt have some understanding of what I mean. Sometimes it seems that all my life has just been stories. And then I wonder sometimes, because now I have more stories than anything else. Maybe what I have waiting for me somewhere on ahead is the opportunity to tell about all the things which have happened to me in my life. And I can tell the stories over and over again, as many times as I want to, and somebody will sit listening to me to the end.

AFTERWORD

Jelly Roll left New York for Los Angeles late in 1940. He had to drive most of the way through blizzard conditions and twice the cars went off the road into the snowdrifts. He reached Los Angeles in very poor health and without money. He continued to write optimistic letters to his wife and managed to send $10 to his sister in June 1941, but collapsed from respiratory difficulties and heart disease and died on July 10. He was fifty-five years old. Following his death Mabel Morton returned to New Orleans. In his will he left his estate to Anita Gonzales.

ACKNOWLEDGMENTS

A number of people talked to me about Jelly Roll and his last months at the Jungle Inn, among them Frederic Ramsey Jr., Charles Edward Smith, Roy Carew, and William Russell. The story of Jelly Roll's encounter with the drummer Herbert Wright was told to me by William Russell. No story about Jelly Roll could be told without acknowledging the debt anyone interested in jazz history has to Alan Lomax, who interviewed him for the Library of Congress sessions in May 1938, and used the material as the basis of his colorful biography of Morton, titled *Mr. Jelly Roll*. A further debt is owed to Harriet Janis, who edited the material for release in a series of twelve albums by Circle Records, and to Rudi Blesh, who as owner of Circle made the release of the records possible. I have taken the liberty of checking Jelly Roll's memories of the Robert Charles riots in New Orleans against the excellent book *Carnival of Fury* by William Ivy Hair, published in 1976 by the Louisiana State University Press, and Jelly Roll's memories of his early days with the traveling theater companies were checked with the book *Nobody, The Life of Bert Williams,* by Ann Charters, currently available as a reprint from Da Capo Press, New York. Also useful were Blesh and Janis's book *They All Played Ragtime,* Martin Williams' *Jazz Masters of New*

Orleans, *Selections From The Gutter*, edited by Art Hodes and Chadwick Hansen, and the introductory note to the music folio *"Jelly Roll" Morton, The Original Mr. Jazz* by Mary Allen Hood and Helen M. Flint. The folio is published by Edwin H. Morris & Company, Inc., and distributed by Charles Hansen, New York.

The photographs opposite pages 19, 36, 110, 126, 140 are by courtesy of Orkester Journalen. Photographs opposite pages 74 and 89 are from the author's collection.